"Toddy Hoare—soldier, sculptor, and parish priest for twenty-five years in rural England. From decades of living close to farmers, and the clay he molds into sculptures, Toddy knows God's creation intimately. Now he fashions the psalms into poems of direct, blunt, cries of longing which speak of God's abiding presence in the chaos of our lives. Both as poetry and spirituality, the psalms speak here afresh as only his rich life could make possible."

—PETER SEDGWICK, former principal, St Michael's College, Llandaff, Wales

"How are the psalms able to capture the whole range of human spiritual experience, from frustration with life and anger at God to exuberant worship and awe at the creation revealed by science? Toddy Hoare provides answers not through prose analysis but through a stunning series of sonnets, one for each psalm and then some. Everyone who reads them—perhaps one-a-day—will be thereby enriched."

—ANDREW BRIGGS, professor of nanomaterials, University of Oxford

"Toddy Hoare's biblical sonnets are disciplined, direct, personal, punchy heart-to-heart conversations with God: 'To study Your Word is my pleasure' (119, ii). He reads the Psalms in Christ and marries Coverdale's antique English with wordplays (42: 'hart . . . heart'), varied rhyming keys and modern vernacular usage: 'discombobulated' (70), 'stink-holes' (69), 'loan-sharks' (109). So now, with Toddy, you could read the Psalter back to front—or travel through the Psalms at speed before reading them in full. What a joy this all is; what a joy the Psalms are; and what a joy God is!"

—PHILIP SEDDON, pastor and theologian

Psalmody

Psalmody

*Thoughts on the Psalms
and Other Matters Spiritual*

TODDY HOARE

Foreword by John Lawrence Pritchard

RESOURCE *Publications* • Eugene, Oregon

PSALMODY
Thoughts on the Psalms and Other Matters Spiritual

Copyright © 2024 Toddy Hoare. All rights reserved. Except for brief quotations in critical publications or reviews, no part of this book may be reproduced in any manner without prior written permission from the publisher. Write: Permissions, Wipf and Stock Publishers, 199 W. 8th Ave., Suite 3, Eugene, OR 97401.

Resource Publications
An Imprint of Wipf and Stock Publishers
199 W. 8th Ave., Suite 3
Eugene, OR 97401

www.wipfandstock.com

PAPERBACK ISBN: 979-8-3852-3596-4
HARDCOVER ISBN: 979-8-3852-3597-1
EBOOK ISBN: 979-8-3852-3598-8

12/22/24

Dedicated to all those who would explore the psalms without guile and others who find ready expression through them in all their forms and guises.

Contents

Lists of Illustrations or Tables | xiii
Foreword by John Pritchard | xv
Introduction | xvii

Section 1. Thoughts on the Psalms (Trust, Help, Deliverance)

1. | 3
2. | 4
3. | 5
4. | 6
5. | 7
6. | 8
7. | 9
8. | 10
9. | 11
10. | 12
11. | 13
12. | 14
13. | 15
14. | 16
15. | 17
16. | 18
17. | 19
18. | 20
19. Language in the Silence. | 21
20. | 22
21. | 23
22. | 24
23. | 25
24. | 27
25. | 28

Contents

26. | 29
27. | 30
28. Intimacy with God. | 31
29. | 32
30. | 33
31. | 34
32. | 35
33. | 36
34. | 37
35. | 38
36. | 39
37. Often I Consider How The Lord Upholds The Pure In Heart. (Beatitudes Anticipated.) | 40
38. Cries To The Lord In Distress. | 41
39. Length Of Years In Vain Without God. | 42
40. | 43
41. Not Out To Give Alms But To Betray (John 13:21–30; 18:2–11). | 44
42. | 45
43. | 46
44. | 47
45. The Bride Becomes The Church. | 48
46. Be Still. | 49
47. | 50
48. | 51
49. Without Hope In Resurrection Life Is Dead. | 52
50. | 53
51. The Sacrifice Of God Is A Broken And Contrite Heart. | 55
52. | 56
53. | 57
54. | 58
55. Betrayal. | 59
56. | 60
57. Poetic Justice In the Wings. | 61
58. | 62
59. | 63
60. We Need Your Unwavering Presence. | 64
61. Intimate Plea To God. | 65
62. | 67
63. | 68
64. | 69
65. | 70
66. Jubilate. | 71
67. For Harvest Festival. | 72
68. | 73
69. Jeremiah's Plea As A Suffering Servant. | 74
70. | 75

Contents

71. | 76
72. Expectations For A Savior King. | 77
73. | 78
74. | 79
75. The Cup Of Judgment. | 80
76. | 81
77. Almost A Reflection By Job. | 82
78. Attend To A Story Of Our National Journey. | 83
79. | 84
80. The Vine Is Uprooted. | 85
81. | 86
82. | 87
83. | 88
84. Thy Amiable Dwellings. | 89
85. God Is Gracious. | 90
86. Almost A Prayer That Might Have Guided And Upheld His Purpose When Jesus Drew Aside To Pray And Escape Hostility And Criticism (Luke 5:16). | 91
87. A Eulogy For The Church. | 92
88. | 94
89. Resurrection In The Offing. | 95
90. | 96
91. As Quoted By Satan When Tempting Jesus In The Wilderness (Matthew 4:6; John 6:15). | 98
92. | 99
93. | 100
94. Vengeance Is Mine: Deuteronomy 32:35; Romans 12:19; Hebrews 10:30. | 101
95. Venite. | 102
96. O Worship The Lord In The Beauty Of Holiness. | 103
97. | 104
98. | 105
99. | 106
100. Jubilate Deo. | 107
101. | 108
102. | 109
103. A Suitable Psalm To Include At A Funeral Service. | 110
104. Consider The Environment, The Waters. | 111
105. | 113
106. This Adds The Conclusion Of How Their Tempting God Unfolded: | 114

Contents

107. | 115
108. | 116
Another Look At 108. Cryptic! Expanding On Moab Is My Washpot, Since Every Name Has A Meaning. | 117
109. | 118
110. | 119
111. The Fear Of The Lord Is The Beginning Of Wisdom (Psalm 112:1; Proverbs 9:10.) | 120
112. | 121
113. | 122
114. | 123
115. | 124
116. The Cup Of Judgment In Psalm 75 Becomes The Cup Of Salvation. | 125
117. | 126
118. | 127
119. | 128
A Summary Of Psalm 119 | 129
120. | 130
121. Most Suitable For A Funeral. | 131
122. I Was Glad When They Said Unto Me We Will Go Into The House Of The Lord. | 132
123. | 133
124. | 134
125. | 136
126. | 137
127. "Nisi Dominus Frustra" Read The Lintel Of Our Yorkshire Vicarage. | 138
128. | 139
129. They Shall Not Benefit From The Blessing "The Lord Prosper You." | 140
130. | 141
131. | 142
132. | 143
133. Unity. | 144
134. | 146
135. | 147
136. His Mercy Endures For Ever. | 148
137. | 149
138. | 150
139. | 151
140. | 152
141. | 153
142. | 154
143. | 155
144. | 156
145. | 157

Contents

146. Matthew 25:31–46 (Called The Judgment). | 158
147. | 159
148. Praise Indeed! | 161
149. A Church's Response. | 162
150. | 163

Section 2. And Other Matters Spiritual. In the Light of Faith.

Spirit of Geology | 169
Myths, Cult and Practice | 170
Considering Prometheus | 171
Apple. Malus Sieversii. | 172
Memorials. | 173
God in the Garden. | 174
Integrity, 1 Peter: Lambeth 2022. | 175
Can AI Have a Soul? | 176
The Funeral of HRH Queen Elizabeth II. | 177
Hospitality. (Stranger at Your Manger.) | 178
Further to Fr Mykhailo Dymyd's Heartfelt Reflection on "Therapy at War. How Can We Heal the Heart of Conflict?" Ukraine. | 179
Memory I. | 180
Memory II. | 181
Memory III. | 182
Spain. After 1482 Alhambra's Changing Ownership. | 183
Cultural Diplomacy. Revealing the Soul of Nations. | 185
Advent. | 186
Advent Scene. | 187
God Displaced. Oxford Martin Discussion on Strongmen in Politics with Lord Patten, Gideon Rachman & Margaret MacMillan. 28/11/22. | 188
Times Change. | 189
Lazarus = Without Help. | 190
Do Dreams Have Destinations? | 191
Four poems based on Bampton Lecture 2022, Oxford University Church, by Prof. Alec Ryrie of Durham University; "The Age of Hitler, and how we can escape it." | 192
The Way of the World. (Apologetics!) | 196

Contents

Prompted Memory. | 197

The Lord's Prayer. | 198

Four Rites of Passage. | 199

Let the Spirit Prompt. | 203

Old York Today. | 204

Temple Worship. | 205

Classical Greece Culture, Olympia | 206

Six Laments for Palestine, one for Ukraine. | 208

There Can Be Hope in Context. | 214

God in His Garden. | 215

Reflection and Familiarization of Isaiah 61:1–11. | 216

Perichoresis—The Divine Dance. (A Hint of Proverbs 8.) | 217

Where Are Faith, Hope And Charity? | 218

Uncovering A Bigger Picture. | 219

Life Everlasting. | 220

What Of The Temple Mount? | 221

Euthanasia I. | 222

Euthanasia II. | 223

Religio: Tethered or Bound? (Matthew 11:28–30.) | 224

Finding The Glory. A Listening Church. | 225

Lists of Illustrations or Tables

Psalm 1. Source of the River Jordan (bottom right) from the snows on Mount Hermon at Banias/Caesarea Philippi.

Psalm 23. A likely spot for baptism in the River Jordan today, below Galilee. 1988.

Psalm 50. Temple Mount from the Mount of Olives. The Golden Dome covers the ancient threshing floor which was a meeting place, a parliament, and a place to encounter God. 1974.

Psalm 61. King David's Tower in Herod's Palace, Jerusalem. 1974.

Psalm 87. Jaffa Gate, Jerusalem. 1974.

Psalm 90. Masada from the East. 1974.

Psalm 107. Ancient shrine to Pan at Banias (Dan) incorporated into Caesarea Philippi and the gate to Hades in the old myths. 1974.

Psalm 124. The foothills of Hermon. A knocked-out Syrian T-54 from the Six Day War. 1974.

Psalm 133. Mount Hermon from the walls of Banias. 1974.

Psalm 147. SW corner of Temple Mount and Al-Aqsa mosque above old gate and washing area. Priests' houses would have been in the foreground. 1974.

Psalm 150. Hezekiah's or the Siloam Tunnel, Jerusalem. Water is ever a theme in the psalms but guarding the water supply

Lists of Illustrations or Tables

was all-important as the well was without the city walls. 2 Chronicles 32:30. 2 Kings 20:20. 750 feet long, hewn by men from both ends at the same time to give access to the Gihon spring (where Solomon had been anointed) when the city was fortified against Sennacharib. 1988.

Psalm 150. Entrance to Hezekiah's Tunnel from city. 1988.

Alhambra Upper Private Palace Gardens, Granada, Spain. 2023.

Olympia, Greece. The spring source was hallowed, bringing water to the area for baths. Site of ancient games, based on martial arts, where participants had to be at peace and those who cheated were pilloried. The race track and arena were to the right, gymnasium and other sports to the left beyond Zeus's and Hera's respective temples. 2024.

SE corner of Temple Mount with foundations of washing/purification area opened up. 1988.

Front Cover: Arab sheep market outside Lion Gate, Jerusalem, from above. 1974.

Rear Cover: Arab sheep market outside Lion Gate, Jerusalem, from the south. 1974.

Most photos taken by me in 1974 with some fighting still on the Lebanese border and Golan Heights around Mt Hermon (a likely spot for the Transfiguration). Others in 1988 by me also. Interestingly enough, my grandfather was one of Allenby's generals at the liberation from the Turks of Jerusalem, December 1917. More recent photos by me to illustrate sonnets not based on the psalms but with a known location.

Foreword

THERE'S A POET IN many of us wondering if he or she could creep out and risk public exposure (praise or ridicule). For people of faith, poetry is our natural language because it's the language of love, the language of the Church and the language of God.

Poetry encourages slow reading. You don't want to rush the process because the gift of the poet is finding the exact right word for an experience and that word is to be savoured and cherished. The words have been selected with great care and deserve respect. Mark Oakley observes that when you buy a book of poetry you may not get many words for your money but you get more meaning for your money.

On the other hand, poetry is often elusive. The words are carefully chosen but they don't attempt to resolve problems, paradox or mystery. They simply lay it out. They don't try to impose meaning. D.H. Lawrence thought that if you try to nail down the meaning of a poem it either kills the poem or the poem gets up and walks away with the nail.

I find I write poetry when a situation demands it because poetry is medicine for hard days. Or, more colloquially, when the going gets tough, the tough write poetry. The Psalmist knew all about hard days and many of the psalms are burdened with problems, pressures and complaints, as well as with the glory, goodness and power of God.

Foreword

Toddy Hoare has taken on the brave task of interpreting the psalms in today's wording and imagery. We are in his debt as he seeks to bring home to us the rugged beauty of the psalms and the powerful emotions behind them—and of other spiritual themes. This is clearly a labour of love and an invitation to engage afresh with the costly truth and wisdom of these ancient texts.

Take your time. Enjoy Toddy's work, and then perhaps find your own blank page and write your own love poem (or complaint!) to God.

+John Pritchard

Introduction

150 SONNETS ON THE 150 psalms plus 55 more sonnets of that ilk on contemporary events and experiences.

The psalms have always been there. "Where is God in any situation?" is a common cry. Sometimes detectable in everyday speech, usually a backbone to acts of worship, often an echo or a *cri de coeur*. At the age of six, living with my grandparents in Dorset, the psalms passed over my head. My grandfather, being the incumbent where Thomas Hardy had been a parishioner but never a resident, allowed me to ring the bells. At the age of eight the psalms seemed an interminable part of Matins at school in Shropshire, but at secondary school in Worcester as a teenager they were slowly absorbed, whether with plainsong or the college choir at full blast singing Psalm 150 at the end of term.

Always I use the Book of Common Prayer with the Coverdale translation of the psalms, with rural hints of the Forest of Dean where Coverdale came from shaping their language. So, while I could not quote whole psalms (we might have learned collects but never psalms at school), subconsciously they have become part of my spiritual DNA and I make no hesitation in using the Coverdale version (familiar to me along with the King James Bible from schooldays) as the text from which I have drawn my sonnets.

I deliberately have not used commentaries, nor therefore given any references, while writing so I could let each psalm speak for itself and try to retain a freshness, even where some psalms might

Introduction

be repetitive. I have added comments and notes from accumulated nuggets of wisdom, and some of my own where I find, for instance, Psalm 32, v2 describing what Nathanael was doing under the fig tree when Jesus saw him (John 1, vv43–51). Not speaking Hebrew, the link was in the old English—"guile."

I do not know them like the back of my hand but when preparing the procession of harvest offerings for the annual Yorkshire Agricultural Society harvest festival, whether in the Yorkshire Minsters, Ampleforth, Trinity Methodist church in Harrogate or a variety of parish churches, the psalms often provided a ready quote for the commentator or the congregational response, item by item. They retain a timeless everydayness.

My main purpose with poetry or sculpture based on scripture, or indeed when preaching, is to try to make people think, to enter a little deeper into spiritual reflection on life, and, hopefully, more readily to find God expecting them. It is interesting to note when reading the gospels how the psalms shaped Jesus' life and ministry. I do include a brief summary of the psalms as separate collections at the end of the book.

Thanks

Thanks must go to Matt Wimer, George Callihan and their team at Wipf and Stock for undertaking the publication of another volume of verse; Ben Jeapes for getting the manuscript ready for them; John Pritchard for his ready support in penning a foreword; those erstwhile endorsers having the confidence to support another volume; and Gay and Peter Hartley, who gave the final sponsorship to oil the press for publication. In the background I must mention Richard Lawrence of Hurst Studio in Oxford, whose friendship and tutoring opened my eyes to lettersetting, printing and the hidden processes that produce a basic book, along with William Sharpington at art school in the late sixties who taught me lettering and introduced me to St Bride's Fleet Street, which became my spiritual home. I mention them both as lettering, lettersetting,

INTRODUCTION

writing poetry and carving headstones are part of a whole. Finally but not least I must mention Liz, my wife, who has to live with my writing poetry, for better or for worse.

End NB

It is worth noting that the psalms (basically hymns) as translated and passed down were antiphonal in that each half verse (either side of the full colon) reflected the other half, so in a sense between priest and people, the latter would seem a chorus in agreement. Furthermore the collected corpus was divided into five books—Psalms 1–41; 42–72; 73–89; 90–106; and 107–150—or even earlier into three—Psalms 1–41; 42–89; and 90–150. Most were for temple worship but some crept in of a more Wisdom background. Some psalms got divided, originally being one psalm (9 and 10; 42 and 43).

Collections were also attributed to a different naming and understanding of God (1–41 were addressed to Yahweh; 42–83 to Elohim.) The sacred name Yahweh meant "*I am who I am*" or "*I will be who I will be*" (Exodus 3:14) so note in the gospels where Jesus says "*I am . . .*" (John 6:35: bread of life; 8:12 and 9:5: light of the world; 10:7: door of the sheep; 10:14: good shepherd; 11:25: the resurrection and the life; 14:6: the way, the truth, and the life; 15:1: true vine; maybe 7:37–38 could claim to be the water of life.) "Elohim" merely means God. Psalms 90–150 were a later, probably Hellenistic period (think Apocrypha) miscellaneous collection.

Furthermore, different psalms were ascribed to or dedicated by different patrons, hence Psalms of David (51–71), Korah (42–49) and Asaph (50, 73–83). Even then, some were muddled and out of place which, no doubt, fits in with the Israelites being taken into captivity in Babylon (597 BC under Nebuchadnezzar II to 538 BC when Cyrus released them), and having to piece together, know, assert and pass on their identity through their story (our scripture) and their worship, incorporating their law and traditions. Post Alexander the Great (356–323 BC) the Jewish traditions were

Introduction

again threatened by a very Hellenized world. The rebuilt temple, post Cyrus's release of the Israelites, had to be rededicated in 164 BC and rebuilt by Herod the Great (20–12 BC), and finished even later, to be destroyed by the Romans in 70 AD in the final Jewish revolt. The last period of Jewish history leading into Jesus's ministry, from the revolt in 166 BC against the dynasty of Antiochus IV, which arose when Alexander's generals divided his kingdom amongst themselves, saw the rise of a dynasty of high priests and of new religious ideas incorporating mediation by heavenly messengers (Word of God), eschatological or end thoughts, messianic hopes of a new kingdom, and resurrection, all of which we find embodied in Christ.

SECTION 1.

Thoughts on the Psalms
(Trust, Help, Deliverance)

Source of the River Jordan (bottom right) from the snows on Mount Hermon at Banias/Caesarea Philippi.

1.

Any man who guards his steps is blessed,
Who disregards scornful judgment when addressed
By critics of keeping true to God's law
Knowing he shall, not them, prosper much more.
The man is blessed who heeds God's Word
Avoiding those who think it's absurd.
The Lord's Way is pleasing, response bears fruit
Prospering tasks in hand watered from the root.
The Lord will blow away the heedless folk
Like chaff scattered on the wind. There's no yoke
For whom no judgment is pending when tried
And the presence of His Chosen isn't denied.
The Lord knows who keep His way (no cost)
But those who follow differently are lost.

2.

Empty thoughts lead nowhere but to fury
When those with power feeling constrained
By God and His Chosen One have opposing vision.
But the Word holds them in derision
Who without faith remain untrained,
With no pleasing sentence before God's jury.
In Sion[1] a proper king is established:
His begotten Son, destined to preach the Word,
Dispossess the heathen, helped start matter.
The earth is His for the asking. He will shatter
All rivals for whom His voice is unheard.
Serve the Lord, give reverence that's relished.
Greet my Son, avoid His displeasure
His anger abates with trust in full measure.

---

1. Sion/Zion = pinnacle, high hill, fortress.

3.

O Lord, how increasingly numerous
Are those who oppose me and have risen
Saying, "In his God he'll find no relief."
You sustain me despite their unbelief,
You are my defense. I call You: listen
And You answered despite their derision.
I slept in peace sure of Your protection.
However outnumbered opposition
Is neutralized as my corner You fight.
Uphold my cause, You accept all who're right.
Pour blessings on Your people and salvation.
Give God glory, Father, Son, Spirit, all three:
Ever and always as one they shall be.

4.

Harken, righteous God, to my call
For You freed me when troubled sorely.
How long will you mortals deride my integrity
And chase after pleasure and vanity?
Be sure the Lord has chosen the godly. If poorly,
Be sure He hears. In your heart, your room withal,
Be still and trust despite detractors.
O Lord, look upon us with abundant grace.
You have made me so glad of heart.
You gave their harvest an increased start.
With kindness You have lifted Your face
Giving confidence with even factors.
In peace I will take my rest and sleep:
You stand guard since it's me You keep.

5.

Ponder on my thoughts, Lord, and prayers
First thing in the morning for wickedness
Is abhorrent, fools have no place, the vain
Stuck where they choose to remain.
I respect You with worship and nearness
Ensures I walk a straight path. Layers
Of deceit, slander, flattery, lies
Mark their rebellion against You.
The destruction they imagine finds voice.
Those who genuinely trust rejoice
Giving thanks, finding joy though few.
Those who love Your name You heed their cries:
A cover of kindness like a shield
Matches the blessings on the healed.

6.

Lord, save Your rebukes however displeased,
Reach out to heal my aches, I am dis-eased.
My soul is troubled, don't punish me more;
Deliver me for of Your mercy I'm sure.
With my death what on earth do You gain?
From the grave do thanks rise with joyful strain?
Fatigued with groaning, my bed soaked with tears,
My countenance has fallen, opposition
Overwhelms me though empty their complaints.
I will throw off their constraints
Confident the Lord has heard my petition
And my cause has reached His ears.
Those against me shall be confounded
On themselves has their hate rebounded.

7.

Lord deliver me from my adversary
I am afraid of being consumed.
I deserve deserts for deception
And betrayal if I'm no exception.
Defend me from actions assumed,
Let not Your judgment vary.
Guide the upright, preserve the true of heart,
Confound the sinner and those who provoke.
From Your scales of justice draw Your sword
To cut off the guilty, give the good reward.
Let those who set a trap miss the joke
When as the victims they fall apart.
Exonerated I will rejoice
And thank the Lord with joyful voice.

8.

"Mornin', Guv."[2*] The best of names reflecting
Glory above all, and exclaimed from birth,
For You're above contradiction.
I look at Your creation, dictation
Of the universe, hand-wrought earth.
Why do You care for man, inspecting
Mankind itself? Below the angels'
Order You raise him in glory
Giving him responsibility
Within the bounds of his ability
Over Your creation's story
As the beginning of Genesis tells.
Land, sea and air You order all
Supreme Governor is our call.

2. A certain verger on opening the church always addressed his maker thus!

9.

With thanks I proclaim God's mighty work
Rejoicing in Your name that You consume
The memorials of vain oppressors.
From Your prepared seat You judge transgressors.
You defend us, for refugees make room
And confound the wretched heathen that lurk
Whom You cause to be caught in their own trap.
Have mercy on me, O Lord, and consider
The trouble I suffer at the hands of others
Because when You save me nothing bothers
And I'm free to sing Your praises wider.
The meek live. In the air I'll throw my cap.
The poor are not forgotten; the upper hand
Denied, mere men are left unable to stand.

10.

I am in need; why do You hide Your face?
The puffed up persecute the poor and boast;
May their own craftiness bring them disgrace.
Your judgments are far, far above the most
That they dare contemplate. Upon their own pate
May fall all they conceive and articulate
For they think God's blind to their inventions
And cares nothing for their machinations.
The poor they wrong upon God depend;
When they cry heathen malice God will end.
What man persecutes those weaker than he?
Who takes God's name in vain is of no account.
They need to know God will be who He'll be,
His grace and majesty are paramount.

11.

I put my trust in the Lord; say no more
I should take flight to the hills like a bird.
When the ungodly arm themselves priming
Their missiles secretly to down the poor
What have the righteous done to deserve
Their establishment's destruction? It's absurd.
You'll find God in His temple with simple timing
Considering the poor, heavenly seat secure.
From supporting humankind He'll not swerve.
He makes room for the righteous, hates the bad
On whom His judgment will fall with brimstone
And worse; adverse to their tricks He's never conned.
The Lord smiles on the deserving alone
Applauds justice but sin He won't condone.

12.

O Lord I need Your help for no support
Is to be found amongst the faithful
Whose numbers have drastically declined.
Others mouth vain things their tongues with lies lined.
They chatter flattery with deceitful
Intentions: make good the butt of their sport.
The Lord will strike dumb those who think they
Have the right to speak and heard above all,
For only His words count so well refined.
To the needs of the comfortless He's not blind:
His Word in good time will prevent their fall
And God indeed shall have the final say.
Rebuking others the heathen strut about
Whose generation won't have the last shout.

13.

Am I forgotten? What game do You play
Of hide and seek? How long do I search
For spiritual guidance to no avail,
A loser, while my gainsayers prevail?
Lord consider my dilemma; I perch
On the brink of death while my enemies say
They have the upper hand. How glad they'll be
To think I'm dejected and they better me.
I rally for I trust in Your mercy
And rejoice that salvation comes from You.
I will sing of God's love, praise Him too.
For all their pettiness there's nothing they do
That debunks the Lord most High from my mind.
I shall enjoy what they can never find.

14.

The fool muses that God does not exist.
Such are rotten, their doings a disgrace.
God scans the whole human race on His list
For any enlightened to seek His face.
But all step aside, avoid doing good;
They express death, speak poison and deceit.
Their speech is foul, they are quick to shed blood.
Destructiveness brings them no joy, no seat
To experience peace or draw near God.
Clueless mischief-makers devour the dear
As the greedy who gobble bread by the wad
But say no grace for they imagine fear
Which in God's generation is wisdom;
They mock people's trust and joy in God's freedom.

15.

Lord, who will spend their days in Your house
Or take their ease on Your holy mount?
Such places are reserved for the uncorrupt
Who perform true and on whom You can count,
Especially those who mind what they say,
Speak no slander and no deceit display.
You include the humble, not the self-important,
Those who keep their word at their own cost,
Those who lend without interest, instant
Honesty without bribes. Those who are lost
You can be sure they do none of these things
Whose lives are run on what falsehood brings.
Whoever walks the Way the Lord has shown
Can count on the place God calls His own.

16.

I'm in Your hands, God, for You hold my trust.
My soul confesses You are my God,
Nothing else I have is of any value.
My example is that the saints have the clue
Whereas those who give false gods the nod
Can expect problems. My choice is a must
Refusing their every oblation,
Of their names I will make no mention,
For the Lord is passed on to me, the cup[3]
Of salvation is the true inheritance
I drink. I'm thankful the Lord holds me up.
In Him I'm certain I find life's true balance
For You spare me hell. From corruption
Your Chosen's spared, joy without interruption.

---

3. See also Psalm 75 where the cup of judgment is offered: also Isaiah, Jeremiah, Ezekiel and Habakkuk.

17.

O Lord hear my complaint; I tell no lie.
I seek Your opinion with equal measure.
You know me, I avoid any offense.
Because some act and speak nonsense
Against You I wait on Your leisure.
Respond to all who on You rely.
Keep me as the apple of Your eye:
Hide me from heathens out to destroy.
Blubber encloses those surrounding me
Waiting in shadow to pounce secretly.
Thwart them, trip them up, Your hand employ.
A fair portion in this life they enjoy,
With heirs to whom they pass their substance old.
When I pass I'll be like You and You behold.

18.

In my distress I will call upon the Lord
Whom I trust. The earth trembles when He descends
His displeasure like a blast that creation rends.
He is holy with the holy who heed His word.
With God's support well trained I will prevail
I shall stand while my enemies fall:
The arrogant topple their hauteur to no avail.
When they cry there is none to aid them all.
The Lord is my light in dark times, my reward
For keeping to His ways, sure footed hart-like.
In God's name I subdue those who dislike
His just rule and reverse their discord.
I thank God my adversaries are disjointed
And He gives prosperity to His Anointed.

19. Language in the Silence.

The heavens declare God's glory; creation
Portrays His skills. The voices of night and day
Call. They have no language but are heard.
You set the daily cycles; the sun will gird
Itself giant-like, a groom on his wedding day.
Nothing hides from its course. My situation
Is governed by God's undefiled law,
Imparted wisdom, and enlightening rule,
Easy guidance to those who unwavering
Serve Him freely with no hint of slaving.
His commands bring joy, a desirable tool
That guards the soul and all reward is sure.
May what I say, my musings and reflection
Be acceptable, Lord, free from correction.

20.

Lord hear another prayer. You dutifully pray
From the very sanctuary of your heart.
I request God to respond to your desire
In answer to your devotions. Don't tire.
In your salvation we have a joyful part
Knowing God's triumph who will stay
His Anointed. While others put their trust
In chariots and horses, weapons of war,
We turn to God and stand when they fall.
Save us good Lord and hear us when we call.
With Your salvation we can ask no more
For we are assured You reward the just.
We show our loyalty in our worship:
Thanks to prayer we cannot slip.

21.

Let the King rejoice ever assured
By Your strength and certain of salvation.
You respond without denying his suit.
With Your crown he lives in good repute.
Blessed with Your joy he serves the nation,
Everlasting felicity his reward.
Your smile lifts up every faithful heart.
There's no miscarriage of justice nor discord
When the King places his trust in the Lord
Whose hand shall cleave your foes apart
Even as a furnace might consume their art:
Their descendants too shall be rooted out
While their intentions will have no clout.
Lord we exalt and praise Your strength without doubt.

22.[4]

My God why dost Thou forsake me, ignore
My case, despite restless pleading day and night?
Our forebears trusted Thee and were proven right.
Despite my trust I am mocked all the more.
Surrounded by such beasts I am disjointed
They broke no bones but pierced my hands and feet;
They part my clothes and cast lots. Deliver me;
My example and praise are ever before Thee
To reveal Thee: hear from Thy mercy seat.
Thou satisfieth the needs of the disappointed.
The poor shall eat and will be satisfied;[5]
Unable to redeem their own souls when they've died.
Expecting worship the Lord governs all nations.
My heirs serve: declare Thee to future generations.

---

4. A strong feature in the crucifixion narratives in the Gospel.
5. Hint of the Beatitudes.

23.

I am certain the Lord is my shepherd:
I want for nothing. In lush pastures
He feeds me, leading me beside streams
To slake my thirst; such comfort redeems.
In His hands and ways my soul matures.
Death stalks in the valleys I walk; You gird
Me, Your crook a symbol of great comfort.
You will set out a table before my foes
To confound them. I am Your selection,
You anointed my head against their rejection.
It's my cup, which You filled to the brim, that goes
To witness of Your favor. Never short
Is Your loving kindness and mercy,
Like being at home, daily following me.

A likely spot for baptism in the River Jordan today, below Galilee. 1988.

24.

The earth is the Lord's; everything about it
Is His. Founded upon the seas it is
Safe from floodwater. Who is worthy
To ascend to the Lord's high place,
To stand before Him in His presence?
Only the unsullied and pure in heart,
Those who are humble, devoid of vanity,
And who do not contemplate deceit.
All in such a category will receive
The Lord's blessing and salvation.
Such righteousness marks all seeking God.
Gates, lift up your heads and let the doors
Open so the King of glory enters in.
Who is He? The triumphant Lord who'll win.

25.

I turn to You, Lord, in You placing my trust.
Don't let me be a loser nor confounded
For there is no shame with hope in Your name;
You'll confuse those whose values aren't the same.
Show me Your ways for Your teaching is rounded
Offering salvation and rescue from the dust.
Please don't remember my sins and offenses
When I was young but let Your goodness guide
Your response, for You show grace to the meek
And encourage others it's You they should seek.
There's reward in keeping the Lord on side.
What person cannot fear the Lord whose senses
Allow him greater ease than God's covenant
Which ensures my comfort and hope is constant?

26.

You're my Judge; I tread an innocent path.
Try me to prove it, Lord. Search my heart.
I follow Your truth, trusting Your mercy.
I do not keep dubious company.
I avoid the wicked, from the bad stay apart.
I'll wash my hands (symbolically a bath
Of inner cleanliness) and so enter
Your sanctuary to give thanks and tell
Of Your great works, since I love Your dwelling.
Please do not confine me with those selling
My life or sinners who do nothing well.
I'll walk in innocence, You're center
To my life, certain of Your protection
So I stand secure in adoration.

27.

How can I fear anyone when the Lord
Saves me and lights my life? When the wicked
Tried to devour me they were tripped up.
Whatever the odds the Lord is my cup.
My main desire is but to rest my head
In God's house and wait upon His Word.
When there's trouble He's my shelter and resort;
He'll sustain me. I'll sing my thanks and praise.
Hear me when I call; answer me. I seek
Thee, don't cast me aside. I remain meek
And dependent when orphaned but You raise
My hopes when falsely accused. I'm not short
Of strength when there is a glimmer of Your
Contract in our world to life underscore.

28. Intimacy with God.

O Lord with Thee I shall share why I'm downcast:
Scorn me not or I'll think Thou doesn't hear
And sink into the grave. Myself I humble
Before Thy mercy seat. Reward not but tumble
Those mumbling mischief makers who bear
Grudges for no reason. They leave me aghast
At their scheming and lack of regard for Thee.
Praise be that Thou heard my plea. Thou reward
My trust and Thou art my sure defense.
I dance for joy at Thy recompense
My hymns are about Thy glory. Discord
Dispersed Thou doesn't disappoint Thy Anointed.
Grant Thy people the inheritance Thou appointed.

29.

Bring sacrificial lambs to the Lord;
Credit Him with worship, His name with strength.
Grant Him all honor due to His name.
He commands the waters, thunder the same.
He rules the seas; glorious is the length
His voice reaches breaking cedars with words;
E'en those of Libanus He makes to skip
Like a unicorn. His voice divides flames
Shaking the very wilderness of earth;
He makes oaks whirl stripping the forests.
He takes His seat above the water floods He tames.
God's honored in His temple for His Kingship
Giving strength to His people and the blessing
Of peace to His chosen His name confessing.

30.

I'll extol Your name, Lord, You keep me standing
Preventing my opposer's success.
You heard my call, healed me and delivered
My soul from hell, from joining the dead.
May saints in praise remember and confess
His holiness. God's wrath lasts no longer
Than the twinkling of an eye; His pleasure
Is found in life, joy replaces depression.
Established by the Lord I am secure.
When God turned away I was bereft:
What benefit am I with nothing left?
Can dust offer thanks or truth express?
Lord have mercy, hear and help; cast anguish
Away so all sing the endless thanks You wish.

31.

I trust You, Lord, hoping that I avoid
Confusion and superstition employed
By those who would ensnare me in their net.
Into Your hands I commend my spirit. Yet
I rely on You when neighbors forgot
Casting me aside like a broken pot.
Show the light of Your countenance: silence
Their lies who speak against whom You select.
Your goodness recompenses those they reject.
You quietly protect Your saints, who have sense
To pray and praise You, from provocation
By their detractors; such preservation
Is the reward of the faithful and all
Who heed Your Word with trust. They shall not fall.

32.

Blessed is anyone who is forgiven!
Blessed all the Lord finds guiltless, without guile.[6]
Failure to confess leaves me out of joint,
My mouth all dry till forgiveness that You point
The faithful towards is realized. While
With You none feel they are drowning. Shriven
I am safe. You teach me the way to go,
The path to tread. Do not be like a beast
Needing a halter for guidance. Given
Wisdom Your disciples will be driven
With new zeal with no fear of the least
Reprimand but with trust every foe
Will be plagued. Mercy and grace surely lift
All righteous hearts with joy—that's God's gift.

---

6. John 1 v43–51; very descriptive of what Jesus found Nathanael doing under the fig tree.

33.

May the faithful sing their thanks accompanied
With instruments for the Lord's Word is true
Which commanded the heavens and gathered
The deep. What He spake was done. He fathered
His people confounding those askew
With devices against hearts He fashioned
In those He considers do understand.
What king can survive on his own reliance
Or be saved by another in alliance?
No horse nor strength deliver from the hand
Of an adversary. The Lord approves
Trust in His mercy, hope that He loves,
So delivers souls, who patiently wait,
From undeserved dearth and death at His gate.

34.

I will ever be thankful to the Lord:
The humble boast assured of His accord.
On those who display integrity
When troubled the Lord will shower pity.
Angels tarry round the fearful to spare
Them. Taste and see how gracious you saints
Will find the Lord always ready to share
His blessings. While the lion for hunger faints
The righteous lack nothing: the countenance
Of the Lord frowns on the evil to weed
Out their very names from all remembrance.
The contrite of heart is saved if in need:
He can count his bones that none are broken.
Certain deliverance is His token.

35.

Plead my cause, take up arms against my foes.
Scatter all my adversaries like dust
Before the wind; leave no grip beneath their toes.
May they be caught in their own trap and bust.
False witnesses discomfort me with lies.
They rewarded with evil my efforts
On their behalf, and denied any ties
Of neighborliness. Such friendship aborts
Trust. How long will You allow such deceit?
Wake up, judge for me. From calamity
Save me: confuse them who enjoy enmity.
Let them be seen and rebuked in the street.
Those who recognise my integrity
Can rejoice and applaud the Lord's pity.

36.

Of those who fear not God I am aware!
Especially the self-important: pride before a fall.
They speak lies, practice deceit, and plot.
In contrast the Lord abhors the lot.
His mercy, righteousness and grace fill all.
The Lord spares and saves: trust His care.
He shares His bounty; drink His pleasure
For it is in His light that we see light.
The Lord's the well of life for creation too.
Don't hold back Your mercy from the true.
Let my adversaries keep away; measure
Their own length and spare my plight.
With You I still stand when You overthrow
The vain who without regard save their ego.

37. Often I Consider How The Lord Upholds The Pure In Heart. (Beatitudes Anticipated.)

Don't let the evil get you down: they'll be
Cut down. Trust the Lord. Do good. Content you've worth.
Commit to Him. Don't fret about those who beneath
Appear to prosper through deviousness.
Don't let them get you in a state but see –
Blessed are the meek: they shall possess the earth.
Peace will refresh the meek: the vain gnash their teeth.
Better the small treasures of righteousness
Than the wealth of the ungodly.
The Lord defends all those who trust and tumbles
The proud. By their own devices He humbles
Those who renege on their debts. The mean
Are soon gone when they appear to flourish,
Jealous that God hears what His elect wish.

38. Cries To The Lord In Distress.

Lord, stay Your anger if I cause displeasure
Since You pierce me anyway and strike me down
Leaving me wounded and groaning, smitten.
You know my wishes: rejection has bitten.
My supporters and family all frown
From a distance while my foes have the measure
Of my woes and leave me deaf and speechless.
Yet still I trust You and You will trip
Those who laugh at misfortune when I slip.
I seem to be in a pandemic, life's a mess,
What wickedness I have I will confess.
While they thrive my enemies cause me stress.
Despite their false rewards don't forsake me:
Hasten to my help, O Lord, and save me.

39. Length Of Years In Vain Without God.

I said, "I will watch my ways and keep guard
Over what I say." I remained silent –
Not even a good word—though painful
With enemies against me pressing hard.
Finally I burst out with anger pent:
How long have I got, Lord? Can I gain, pull
A longer span otherwise life seems vain?
We walk in Your longevity's shadow.
Who will inherit what a man builds up?
When I ask what is my hope it is You.
Spare me from myself, I am struck dumb.
When You chasten a sinner his glory
Evaporates, moth-eaten, mere vanity.
As on someone passing through show pity.

40.

Waiting patiently I learned the Lord heard,
Pulling me from the pit to firm ground
Putting a new song in my mouth, witness
To others whom, guileless, the Lord will bless.
Your handiwork even as men have found
Is greater than I can say. But Your Word
Is our guide: not sacrifices but Your law
Is fulfillment and I'll declare it loudly.
I have declared Your righteousness of yore
As continuous to the Church, and proudly
Proclaimed Your mercy. I'm content with my lot:
Don't abandon me to my supposed sins.
Rebuke those denying me that none wins;
By my redeemer I'll not be forgot.

41. Not Out To Give Alms But To Betray (John 13:21-30; 18:2-11).

Blessed is the almsgiver, The Lord has his care,
Even preserving his life when vexed sore.
For comfort from sin I seek forgiveness.
Others wish me ill, anticipate less
My recovery, my demise is sure.
Let their lies be their sentence, their share
Of guilt condemn them. E'en my bosom friend
Breaks my trust, who ate with me now waits
To betray me. Raise me in Your mercy
So they receive my reward. Restore me
To display Your favor that he who hates
Cannot triumph over those You defend.
Hale and hearty I'll stand before Your face;
Blessed be the Lord for His loving grace.

42.

As the hart seeks water so my heart yearns
For Your presence, God. When shall I appear?
I went to Your house with the congregation
But was alone in my praise and thanksgiving.
What causes anxiety, troubling the soul?
Trust in God for kindly He looks down.
I remember promises You made at Jordan,
On Hermon too. Depth to deep calls, like noise
From waterfalls cascading down mountains,
Billows that engulf, reminding us God's own
Promises hold true. His salvation maintains
Me when people mock. He steadfast remains.
What causes anxiety, making the soul sigh?
Trust in God, before His face I hold my head high.

43.

Judge in my favor, against deceitful
Detractors defend me, God. Pitiful
I rely on You but You seem so distant.
With such heavy going I begin to pant.
You leave me wading with difficulty.
Shine in my darkness; me Your truth will guide
Into Your high dwelling and sanctuary
Where I know I'll find joy and gladness.
I'll sing hymns to dispel my sadness.
I will thank my God in whom I abide.
While I am discomforted and sad
Remove such disquiet to leave me glad.
What causes anxiety, making the soul sigh?
Trust in God, before His face I hold my head high.

44.

We have heard through the generations
What You did in their time, how You drove out
Heathen peoples and planted our forbears,
Whom You favored. You are my King who hears
Our cries for help. We cannot win a bout
Against our enemies. Your interventions
Give us the upper hand. That is our boast.
But now You appear to have deserted us;
Before our adversaries we are shamed,
Turning our backs to run away and blamed
As cowards when neighbors start to discuss
Our plight. We keep Your covenant the most
For we don't forget God who knows our heart
Even when slaughtered like sheep for our part.

45. The Bride Becomes The Church.

My pen is poised, so to speak, to compose
Good things about God, arbiter of truth,
Meekness and righteousness, who hates
Iniquity. He wields His scepter, indicates
His support for the bride lavishly couth,
Destined as consort of the king He chose.
Beautifully attired with character to match,
With maids of honor of royal stock,
She pleases God whom worship will enhance;
Joy and gladness shall precede her entrance
To the King's palace. As chip off the old block
It makes her as bearer of children a catch
For Thy name in future generations
To be remembered by thankful nations.

46. Be Still.

God is our hope and strength: a present aid
When troubles strike. Whether landslide, earthquake,
Tempest or flood we shall have no fear.
The rivers fill God's city with good cheer.
He's in the center so nothing can shake
Her. God will help in His good time
Kingdoms come and go not His creation:
God is our refuge but brings destruction
On those who hold Him in no regard.
He brings peace, weapons of war He'll discard,
Chariots and armor will be halted.
Be still and know that I am God, exalted
By the heathen in time and on the earth.
The Lord of hosts is our refuge from birth.

47.

Come on everyone, clap your hands,
Sing and make melody. The Lord is high
Above, to be respected above all kings.
He subdues nations we tread on and brings
Us a choice heritage, e'en amplify
Our descent from Jacob in these lands.
God ascends merrily, blow the trumpet,
Sing His praises. He rules, we understand,
All creation. Even the wretched heathen
Are His subjects; from His throne He then
Judges them. Princes mingle, go hand in hand
With those who claim spiritual debt
As Abraham's descendants; God will wield
To defend the earth His mighty shield.

48.

Great is the Lord, and highly to be praised:
Especially on Sion's Temple Hill
Overlooking the city from a place
To the north of great David's fair palace,
A refuge to all, where earth's kings are still.
In their astonishment strange fears are raised
Suddenly like a woman's birth pangs strike.
The Lord's power can arouse the east gale
To shatter ships at sea as we believe,
Waiting on God in the knowledge we'll receive
His world-wide loving-kindness without fail.
His judgments are what Sion's daughters like.
Encompass Sion and mark well her defense.,
God is our guide all generations hence.

49. Without Hope In Resurrection Life Is Dead.

Harken to some wisdom everyone:
I'll listen to parables and truth confess.
What point is there trusting riches and wealth?
None can free his brother nor bargain his health
With God; redemption of souls is priceless
So leave it however long you live on.
All perish thinking their line will endure
Even when they call estates by their name.
Here's folly; all die like fauna for sure.
Beauty doesn't last in the grave nor fame,
However happy: do good is my role,
Then to receive me God delivers my soul.
Have no fear, the self-made man cannot keep
Possessions when silenced and asleep.

50.

The Lord speaks appearing out of Sion
Summoning all who keep as His scion
His covenant, for the heavens declare
His righteousness to judge and refuse
Animal sacrifices to appease;
Rather thanksgiving sacrifices will please.
For those wrongdoers there's no excuse,
Who slander, steal, cheat and falsely swear,
Who preach God's laws which they plainly reject,
Unreformed hypocrites that they are.
I'm to blame if I don't reprove those who forget:
I will pluck them away. To those honoring
Me with thanks, praise and consideration
I will show and offer my salvation.

Temple Mount from the Mount of Olives. The Golden Dome covers the ancient threshing floor which was a meeting place, a parliament, and a place to encounter God. 1974.

51. The Sacrifice Of God Is A Broken And Contrite Heart.

In Your great mercy wipe clean my slate:
Cleanse me of sin which I humbly admit.
Was my conception in a fallen state?
Inner integrity I won't omit.
Purged with hyssop, whiter than snow, my fate
Is hearing joy and gladness without limit.
Ignore my mistakes, clean heart reinstate,
Renew within me a right spirit.
Don't dump me, Your holy Spirit is great
Comfort and my way forward will be lit.
I'll teach sinners Your ways, Your law relate
In return for health and spared from the pit.
I open my mouth with praise, knowing You
Won't despise my contrite sacrifice too.

52.

The bully boasts, his tongue talks terrible tricks,
His lies slash like a razor. He prefers
Unrighteousness in contrast and picks
Quarrels opposite to one who prefers
God's goodness that daily endures unworn.
It's God who'll pluck him out from house and home;
His name shall cease and he'll be laughed to scorn
By the righteous. He preferred to roam
His own domain secure in his standing
Rather than trust God to give real reward.
Since I know God's tender mercy's landing
In my lap for free I don't play the fraud.
I feel like a fresh green olive tree placed
In God's atrium by no means disgraced.

53.

Only a fool reckons there is no God.
Such people are corrupt doing evil.
God looks down searching if mankind might show
Those who seek Him all the better to know
Truth and honor but is disappointed. Nil
Score points: His way remains neglected, untrod.
His people are an abomination
Consuming all before them as if food,
Despicable before the God they ignore.
He has shattered your enemies for sure
So you can scatter them doing no good.
May Israel experience salvation,
Even deliverance from captivity,
Rejoicing become their activity.

54.

Save me O Lord as I call upon Thee:
I rely on Thy strength to avenge me.
Hear my prayer, let my cries reach Thy ears.
Those I don't know are the cause of my tears;
Veritable tyrants whose terrible acts blind
Them to God whose constancy I call to mind.
He is my helper, with those lending support,
Rewarding their evil spoiling their sport.
Thy truth O Lord is their own destruction.
Freely I offer my heart as oblation
For praise and thanks make me comfortable:
Now released from trouble as He is able
I noticed God worked His will in His way
Upon those who oppose and try to waylay.

55. Betrayal.

O Lord hear my prayer, don't ignore me.
My detractors are hot on my heels
Seeking to do me mischief. I am ready
To drop. Full of dread my head reels.
O for the wings of a dove that I might
Fly to find refuge and rest in flight
Away from storm and tempest since I spied
Strife in the city while my foes have tried
Stirring up trouble: for their opposition
Is hidden. Where their mischief was open
I could have ridden the situation;
But it was my friend, trust in him broken.
With buttered words he broke God's covenant
But I pray he'll regret that he did recant.

56.

Be merciful unto me, O God, I cry
For I am an innocent victim yet
Despite their daily endeavors my trust
Remains with You. Constantly they just
Misrepresent what I say; in Your debt
I'm secure. You know my flittings, why
I am downtrodden. I know that You will
Chase them all away, cast them all aside,
Vent Your displeasure and give me comfort.
Against my trust they will have no retort:
God is on my side, in Him I abide,
Finding comfort however hard they try.
I walk, stand secure, God's delivering
Ensures I'm in the light of the living.

57. Poetic Justice In the Wings.

However much people may gainsay me
Criticizing and mocking my faith:
Rather than I be a victim of their reproof
God'll reprove them for their words are uncouth,
Piercing in extreme need I saith!
They set a trap to trip me but maybe
They fall in the pit they have dug.
They deserve more than poetic justice!
My trust vindicates me, I will not miss
Opportunities to give thanks; I hug
The path of the Lord, I strike up a song
To attract attention to God among
The people so they in turn will proclaim
His mercy and glory o'er earth remain.

58.

Are you folk focused on righteousness?
Are you judging their correct behavior
When others imagine mischief and devise
Devious handiwork? Where intentions
Are not to be trusted each perpetrator
From birth has been a basket of lies,
A snake beyond the power of the best
Charmer. Chuck them from Your presence
That instead we may enjoy their absence.
Let them melt like a snail that dissolves in salt.
May Your fierce indignation be aroused
As a fire of thorns heats a pot. Vengeance
Exists; the evidence of their treatment
Shows all men justice at Your hands is meant.

59.

O Lord rise to my help for I am hounded
Without reason. Deliver me; doglike, huge,
They wait to pounce and catch me out. Unfounded
Is their spurious allegation;
Your laughter can hold them in derision
For You are my strength and refuge.
Scatter rather than slay them lest people
Forget their false preachings which with lies ring.
Consume them that all may know that You rule
Our hearts and thoughts lest they transition
Like a stray pack to find satisfaction
For their lifestyle which I abhor. I sing
Of Your power and strength; Your mercy
Is my defense wherein lies security.

60. We Need Your Unwavering Presence.

O God, Thou hast thrown us out and dispersed
Those of us who thought we were special.
Thou hast been displeased but please change Thy mind.
The earth shakes and land is divided we find.
Difficult things in an ongoing serial
Have been witnessed and we appear cursed
By Thy cup of judgment.[7] But Thy token
To those who trust promises victory.
Deliver Thy beloved and subdue
Those around whose loyalty is overdue.
Their subjection will count as Thy glory:
All showing acceptance will not be broken.
We need Thy help. Man is unreliable.
With Thee enemies will find us terrible.

---

7. Imagery of the cup of judgment in the OT becomes cup of salvation (Psalm 116) in the NT and at Holy Communion. See also Psalms 16, 27, 60, 75 in relation to Matt.26:39-45, and Mark and Luke.

61. Intimate Plea To God.

O God, I'm disconsolate. My prayer
Is before Thee. From the ends of the world
I would make my petitions when my heart
Is burdened asking that Thou make a start
To set me up on firm ground, with unfurled
Wings to cover me with a layer
Of Thy protection in which I trust
As if dwelling in Thy sanctuary.
I know my desires have reached Thee
Which Thou dost grant as to all who fear Thee.
The heritage Thou dost offer doesn't vary.
Thou hast gifted the King long life, more than just
Beyond his own generation. Preserve
Him with Thy mercy since it's Thee I serve.

King David's Tower in Herod's Palace, Jerusalem. 1974.

62.

I hang in there with God as He ensures
Salvation. As for those who denigrate
Me they shall collapse like an unstable wall.
They want any whom God favors to fall
Being hypocrites who initiate
Lies. Despite all, my hope that God abhors
The vain, who like false weights, are lighter
Than the deceit and scams they spread about.
They may get rich, trust not but watch out.
God repeats to Him belongs all power:
Mercy on the faithful He will shower.
Men trusting God find their rewards brighter
According to how He assesses their work
And responsibilities they don't shirk.

63.

O God, my God, early each day I seek
Thee as one parched in waterless wastes.
I sought Thy holiness that I might see
Thy power and glory. My mouth praises Thee
For Thy mercy exceeds more than life tastes.
I stretch to praise Thy name for I am meek.
My joyful worship is rewarded; the best
Falls to me as my waking moments turn
My prayers to Thee as my sure helper
In whose very shadow I find shelter.
I depend on Thee so let my foes learn
They shall be buried, struck at Thy behest
With the sword's edge to be food for fox and vermin.
Loyalty will the King commend and determine.

64.

Preserve me, O God, from that bunch of foes
Rising in their deviousness against me.
Hide me, their words are biting and hurtful:
Their pot shots of slandering are painful.
Amongst themselves they plot iniquity,
Planning methods to trip the good but pose
Their own innocence. Suddenly God will
Catch them unawares and strike them all down.
Yes their own speech will be their undoing:
Those who notice will laugh with much booing.
Their scorn will credit God whose very frown
Confused them and brought their purpose to nil.
Those trusting the Lord have cause to rejoice:
Gladness of heart shall give them tuneful voice.

65.

Your praise is found in Zion, Jerusalem
Is the destination for the loyal.
All will turn to God and vows He will hear
Despite the burden of misdeeds we bear.
Those You choose and accept in Your royal
Dwelling are blessed where they'll find pleasures stem.
The God of our salvation reveals things
Too wonderful to behold: the mountains
Are raised tall by Him, storms at sea are stilled,
Disturbed people calmed. Distant folk are filled
With awe that after dark the sun remains
To return another day; harvest brings
The bounty of the earth, and waters pull
Fertility so fields and folds are full.

66. Jubilate.

O be joyful in our God all ye lands,
Such wonderful works happen at His hands.
Those who discredit Him will be found out
For seeing what He has done removes doubt.
We crossed the sea on dry land and exulted,
Reduction of disbelievers resulted.
Praise our God who keeps our feet from slipping
Who proved us in times past even tripping
As a test before leading us somewhere
Pleasant to settle and build Your house there.
Here we placate God with the sacrifice
He desires but tell all who would entice
Folk with falsehood that God is deaf to such
But in thanks for His mercy I make much.

67. For Harvest Festival.

We ask God for His blessing and mercy
That His radiance might be obvious;
That His ways on earth might be revealed;
Make all aware His salvation can yield
Good health to those others oblivious
To His power in creation we see.
This is cause for rejoicing on a scale
For all to share and acknowledge He's fair
When judging and that He governs nations
Righteously restoring relations,
Bringing harmony and peace, a pair
To celebrate and enjoy without fail.
In response to our praise creation brings
Plentiful harvests and all God's good things.

68.

God scatters His foes like before the wind
Smoke disperses or wax melts in the heat.
He's Father to the fatherless, no less,
Supporter of widows. Let the earth tremble
For before Him men do not dissemble.
He gives out His Word that all might possess
Truth. The company of preachers is great
The Heavenly Host's innumerable men find.
God brings His people through tribulation
Who respond in processions of thankfulness.
The vanquished pay tribute in their defeat
When God restores stability from mess
And sets His chosen back on their feet.
Recognise that power belongs to God,
Let us find peace following where He trod.

69. Jeremiah's Plea As A Suffering Servant.

Save me O God from this stink-hole's rising
Filth ere I drown. If I've misled any
I apologize. It wasn't my intention
To misrepresent Thy intervention.
Those who understood aren't the enemy:
Be lenient, I pay with suffering.
I am dishonored and rejected, the butt
Of their ribaldry. I find no pity
Save in Thee. I'm given vinegar to drink
As torment for thirst. I'm inclined to think
They should come to grief; they take the city
Wealth for granted. May they choke on their glut.
Let the poor and downtrodden take note and do
What pleases the Lord to posterity renew.

70.

Lord make haste to help, make speed to save me.
Shame those who wish all misfortune on me,
Who'd like to see me discombobulated.
Since the harm they wished on me escalated
Their hopes to bring me down increased greatly.
Instead hoist as their own victims may they be.
Reward them with shame that soothe falsely,
But those that seek You honestly find joy
And true gladness in the reality
Of Your salvation and rescue. Now see
Our helper and redeemer and employ
Your best prayers to lift my misery.
Praise the Lord. Delight in security
The Lord upholds all on whom He has pity.

71.

Lord in You I put my trust entirely
Dependent on Your deliverance.
Confound those opposing me who doubt
My faith in You and put falsehoods about.
In Your strength I stand, trusting You my stance,
From the first at birth You have supported me,
And remained true but I am odious
In the sight of others who seek to catch
Me out. I speak of Your righteousness
Intending to go out in Your strength. Bless
Me with enough years to show You, despatch
Me not before I show You are gracious
To the next generations that follow
And how what You promise is not hollow.

72. Expectations For A Savior King.

Grant the King wisdom in making judgment
And more to his son to defend the poor.
He shall enable their focus on the good,
Righteousness will last as long as the flood
In olden times till the world no longer endure.
His abundant peace shall be permanent.
His foes and all kings will make obeisance
Offering gifts and to do great service.
Just shall be His gentle rule, the poor preserved,
Petitions heard, verdicts given as deserved.
Gold and the fruits of the earth beyond price
Mark His benefits. Prayer in His presence
With praise will gain future posterity,
All the Lord could do for their prosperity.

73.

Relationship to God never sever
But understanding His Word endeavor.
God supports the true of heart but we slide
While the ungodly appear to prosper.
Where is their misfortune? Why so much pride?
People fall for the promised earth they foster.
They think God doesn't know so enjoy their wealth.
I despair, innocent hands, pure in all
While they gain the upper hand.
The way of the world is hard to understand
Until I stood before God and saw them fall,
Their image vanished as dreams with dawn's stealth.
God upholds the just and don't I know it;
Even when things are bleak I'll not show it.
To spurn God is a missed situation
Yet I declare God gives true salvation.

74.

Why, God, have You deserted us? Are You angry?
Don't forget us whom You saved to Your cost.
Consider us or Your inheritance lost
While we are shouted down, driven astray.
They have trampled our emblems to lift their own.
Whilst the craftsman carved wood in Your honor
They chop it up, destroying panels and door,
Burning Your sanctuary, Your house pulled down.
We've no prophet, this is beyond our ken,
You can help us as before, we wonder when.
Your power divided the sea, dried water here
Flushed water from the hard desert rock there.
Shame not the simple, fight Your corner, defend
From the presumptive all who on You depend.

75. The Cup Of Judgment.[8]

We thank You, God; Your works declare You're close.
When in charge I shall judge rightly; people shift,
They're weak so I hold them up. I tell fools
To keep Your covenant, observe the rules;
Beware of pride, shun haughtiness. No lift
In life is to be found for the morose.
God is judge as He says and He decides
Who to promote or put down. Their merits
Are weighed. He holds a cup full of red wine
From which He pours: for the elect it's fine,
The ungodly get the dregs. Their spirits
Fall short and instead it's them God derides.
Thus I say God's judgment is fair, the proud
Toppled, the faithful with salvation endowed.

---

8. A theme of psalmists and prophets that becomes the cup of salvation (Psalm 116) through Christ at Communion.

76.

Jews experience and know God's great name
Since Jerusalem is His sanctuary.
There He shattered enemy weaponry;
The city is stronger than robbers who came.
The proud are stripped, there's nothing in the grave:
The God of Jacob puts cavalry to flight.
When He's angry who can stand in His sight?
His very judgment defies even the brave.
God stills the trembling earth to help the meek.
He turns any who with wrong intent seek
Him from passion to praise: He doesn't save
The brutal and shuns fanatics who rave.
Keep your promises, bring gifts of respect,
His influence on kings is good to reflect.

77. Almost A Reflection By Job.

I will cry to God. It could be my sobs
Will attract His attention to heed me.
Day and night I explained my trouble
When my life collapsed like a heap of rubble.
Now I question Him, does He need me?
I remember good times past. Absence robs
His promises and mercy from my mind:
Only His displeasure is all I find.
I will think of Your doings and past works
For You are holy and do wonders.
My heart Israel's deliverance ponders,
How the waters re-acted, Your force that jerks
The earth. You are sea-borne; no steps on land
Were seen when You directed Moses' hand.

78. Attend To A Story Of Our National Journey.

Walk with me; I'll remind you our story
Concerns the covenant with Jacob, law
And trusting God in spite of our relapse.
That journey of escape from Egypt taps
Into our own experience, a door
Revealing God's might, care and glory.
He commanded waters to part, or to spring
From the rock. A series of disasters,
Each culminating from the last, enabled
Escape. Yet forgetting our debt, now fabled
How we choked on the meat we craved, masters
Our decline from favor when God would bring
Release and a new lease of life. He chose
David: from the temple His love for us goes.

79.

Thy temple is a heap of rubble while heathen
Trample down the ruins and trouble Your chosen.
Why are You angry? What is it we've done?
Instead pour out on them Your indignation
Since they mock us and shame Your holy name.
Salvation comes from You: if we're to blame
Have mercy upon us and bring revenge
On those who taunt us for our lack of You.
Their blasphemy deserves hard punishment:
Exert Your power else they won't relent.
Prisoners' sorrowful sighs please review
Ere their doom is sealed which we can't avenge.
Vindicated we'll be ever grateful
As sheep of Your pasture with praises full.

80. The Vine Is Uprooted.

Hear our cries O You, our Shepherd, Your sheep
Are scattered. How long will Your anger last?
We drink our own tears. We are laughed to scorn.
From Your protection and care we are torn.
Let clouds hiding Your countenance scud past.
The vine planted from Egypt needs You to keep
It safe and fruitful: it is desolate,
Unprotected and plucked by passers-by.
Wild boars root it up, and of no avail
Its former spread against such a trail
Of destruction. Look and feel You must try
To rescue this vine: close the vineyard gate,
Establish Your Son. We'll make amendments
Awaiting Your smile as Your dependents.

81.

Bring out the instruments and sing.
God bade us a feast day to celebrate
Our exodus and our deliverance
In times past giving our mother tongue a chance
To be heard. No more making pots our fate.
Our woes were changed to a much better thing.
Hear our God, no more forced to worship strange
Gods He will feed us if we would obey.
But no; we followed our own devices and
Desires regardless and defied the hand
That restored our freedom. It made God stay
His intentions and interventions; arrange
Instead for us to miss the fat of the land,
Choice honey extracted from rocks and sand.

82.

God is in the company of rulers:
He is ultimate Judge of all surely!
How long will you favor. the wrong persons
And defer to them not the innocent?
Our duty is to the unfortunate,
The orphan and widow, and to right wrongs
Against any outcast who for rights longs.
How long will You allow injustice to last?
Rulers fail to see our environment
Is topsy-turvy and walk in darkness.
The world is out of sorts, establishment
Undone. Despite my saying you're the sons
Of God you are mortal and will die.
Arise, Lord, restore justice and firmness,
Subject the heathen in their stubbornness.

83.

Don't hold Your tongue, God, foes are murmuring
Against You and to bring us to nothing.
Their confederation is taking counsel
With all round our borders to sponge Israel
From the map and be dismembered.
Our name no more to be remembered.
Arise God to scatter them as You foiled
Our foes long ago, their aggression spoiled,
When You drove Midian's ranks from our land,
Even Sisera at a woman's hand.
Now to those coveting our possessions
Thwart them in their guilty aspirations.
Make them walk round in circles, like stubble blow
Them away so Your might and Name they know.

84. Thy Amiable Dwellings.

How we love Thy churches and holy places!
We long to enter through those ancient doors
Rejoicing in a God who is alive.
Sparrows perch inside, swallows arrive
To nest and lay their eggs. Thy altar ensures
A safe home where blessings cheer our faces.
Blessed the person who finds strength in Thy ways,
Whose faith in Thee draws comfort from Thy grace
As from a well in barren circumstances
Shedding worries about facing adverse chances.
It's preferable to be Thy doorman than face
Life where heathen dwell. To pass a thousand days
Cannot better one day in Thy courts whence
We know Thou art our light and sure defense.

85. God Is Gracious.

O Lord by Thy graciousness we are
Delivered, our sins forgiven for sure.
Please forget Thy wrathful indignation
And set aside Thy angry displeasure.
Show Thy mercy: grant us Thy salvation.
Set us on the right path not a way far
From Thee lest we upset Thee again.
I will take note and listen carefully
To what the Lord might say concerning me.
He will speak peace that His people remain.
Our plenty stems from His loving kindness.
Mercy and truth conjoin: righteousness
Kisses peace. Respect God that His glory
Dwells in our land and truth is His story.

86. Almost A Prayer That Might Have Guided And Upheld His Purpose When Jesus Drew Aside To Pray And Escape Hostility And Criticism (Luke 5:16).

O Lord, bow down to hear me properly;
Let me share my misery for I'm holy.
For comfort I will call on You daily
Trusting in Your goodness when humbly
I seek Your mercy and graciousness.
O God I appreciate Your uniqueness,
Your creativity is matchless
So all will seek Your righteousness.
I am grateful and will worship Your name
For in Your mercy You remove all blame.
Lord, the proud who delight in their own fame
Abuse me: in Your mercy bring them to shame
As a token to me, son of Your handmaid,
And others will see Your comfort displayed.

87. A Eulogy For The Church.

Built upon selected hills Jerusalem
Is the object of the Lord's affection
And choice. God has established His seat
That His chosen extol Him when they meet.
His church of His past deeds make mention
That in order to plant a mother stem
For the birth of His community
He overcame all local hostility.
It will be plainly written in His book
That Zion is the genesis He took
To Himself to found and inaugurate
A people for His pleasure and demonstrate
His love for His creation when they sing
Of His provision of everything.

Jaffa Gate, Jerusalem. 1974.

88.

O Lord God please come to my rescue!
Hear my prayer else I will land in Hell;
I am dismissed as one who's as good as dead,
Forgotten as already in the grave.
You have separated me from friends who dread
My name. There's no rescue from prison: save
Your servant. Can the dead rise up and tell
Of wonders beyond the grave You might do?
If I'm destined below for destruction
Is anyone there to hear my witness?
What good is it if Your righteousness
Is forgotten, Your wondrous works get no mention?
Why do You cast me aside? Misery
Engulfs me, and my bosom friends spurn me.

89. Resurrection In The Offing.

Always shall my song celebrate Your truth
To younger generations: Your mercy
Endures. With David I made a covenant
Establishing his throne for heirs extant.
Who can be compared to God? Raging sea
Is stilled; You scattered Egypt the uncouth.
The heavens and the round world You founded
Belong to You. Equity is Your seat.
Blessed are those walking in Your ways, Your light
Is their delight, Your protection their right.
I anointed my servant David: I beat
His foes. In My mercy he is grounded.
He shall call me Father. He's my first-born.
Why You have forsaken him? He's forlorn.
[9]Who can live and not die? Or deliver
His soul from hell? You are the life giver.

---

9. To make sense of the last ten lines I have had to add two more!

90.

Lord You have been our refuge through the ages.
You were before time and continue forever.
Man may be destructive; You summon him.
A thousand years pass like yesterday's whim.
Man fades away like the grass and never
Remembered. We devour, deserve Your rages.
We may live threescore years and ten even
Fourscore but the going is hard, soon passed.
We need to respect Your displeasure: teach
Us to number our days, the heart of each
To learn wisdom. Stop our being harassed.
Satisfied with Your mercy we're given
To rejoicing and comfort is our perk.
Your Majesty prospers our handiwork.

Masada from the East. 1974.

91. As Quoted By Satan When Tempting Jesus In The Wilderness (Matthew 4:6; John 6:15).

Blessed is the person under Your protection.
My response to God Almighty, "My trust
Is placed in You, my hope and stronghold."
God delivers you from dangers of old
Sheltered like a chick as mother hen must.
God's faithfulness is your preservation,
His trust is your guard. He removes all fear:
You will escape attempts on your life, plague,
Death in battle, but witness these as reward
For the ungodly. Defense is in the Lord.
No way is His grace and mercy vague.
His angels have charge over you and bear
You up lest you trip. "His call I shall hear
And I'll deliver one whom I hold dear."

92.

There's nothing better than to thank the Lord,
To set praise to song early each day,
For His love and His honesty each night.
Your works are glorious, intentions right.
The stupid fail to consider His way:
The dopes' folly won't comprehend His Word.
When the naive and the wicked flourish
They shall be cut down, the unjust perish.
I shall be raised up, with oil anointed.
I shall witness His zeal for my defense.
And listen to His desires and good sense
For my preservation. He's appointed
His chosen to enjoy plenty, to show
Evidence of His strength on earth below.

93.

The King has dressed in His best finery,
Attired with power. Challenge Him who dares!
He set the round world on firm foundations:
It can't be shaken nor change its stations.
He's from the very beginning and prepares
His throne. His directions are very
Certain for He's also everlasting.
Our meditations ascertain His rule
Over the elements that even floods
Can't prevail whatever their raging moods.
The Lord on high is mightier. A fool
Dismissing His reign may be questioning
But His testimonies waver never:
Holiness becomes His house forever.

94. Vengeance Is Mine: Deuteronomy 32:35; Romans 12:19; Hebrews 10:30.

Vengeance belongs to God. As Judge show
Yourself: requite the proud as they deserve.
How long will those who disdain us and smite
Your chosen have the upper hand? It's not right:
They think You don't notice. They have a nerve!
Shall not He who made all our senses know?
The Lord knows who nurtures disharmony.
You give the blessed patience in adversity.
The Lord will not forsake His promises for
Righteousness and judgment to favor
His saints. Who supports my necessity
Against those who treat with acrimony
The Lord's select? He comforts those maligned
By the hostile: to nought they are consigned.

95. Venite.

O come, let us sing praise unto the Lord.
Our salvation calls for celebration,
Demanding thanksgiving in His presence.
The Lord is a great God; it's an offense.
Pretending otherwise. Fabrication
Of the elements and the world accord
Him complete mastery. He holds the earth
In His hands which prepared the dry land.
Let's kneel before our Maker in worship.
We are His sheep in His pasture. Don't slip
Into old ways provoking Him. Understand
Our fathers' temptation led to a dearth
Of God's support. He forbade their sharing
His sabbath without knowing His ways showing.

96. O Worship The Lord In The Beauty Of Holiness.

Come and sing unto the Lord a new song.
Tell of His greatness and our salvation.
Wise up the ignorant about His wonders.
Heathen gods are mere idols: who ponders
Their ability? There's nowt they fashion!
But God made the heavens and nothing wrong.
Ascribe to God His due and acknowledge
His power with praise. O worship the Lord
In the beauty of holiness. In awe
We stand. Tell unbelievers what's in store:
How He made the world secure; He's adored
By creation. To all people He makes a pledge
To judge the faithful with righteousness
But confound the undeserving's stubbornness.

97.

How glad is the earth that the Lord is King!
Surrounded by clouds and darkness His lightnings
Scatter His foes before His justice seat.
Even the world trembles, hills melt with His heat.
The heavens declare His glory: dawnings
And evenings with colors echoing.
As for those who worship carved images
Delighting in their empty vanity
They shall learn the Lord is reality
Above them all and that throughout the ages
He has preserved all who eschew evil.
All rejoice that He combats the devil.
A new light for the righteous has dawned:
Remember He's holy, heathens be warned!

98.

Come. Sing your thanks to the Lord of all
For the marvelous things He does. His hands
Deliver victory. His mouth declares
Salvation. He has toppled the unawares
And demonstrated His truth in all lands.
So be joyful, players answer the call:
Bring instruments, sing hymns of thanks,
Tune your harps, blow your trumpets, groups and bands
Orchestrate to music a happy song.
Let the sea take up the chorus along
With dwellers in the round world: clap your hands
In time that hills echo and riverbanks.
The Lord comes to judge the earth and reveal
His ways of righteousness with His seal.

99.

The Lord is King. The people clamor aloud
In a fever of excitement when God
Mounts His throne. They give thanks to His name
As wonderful, mighty, holy. His fame
Dwarfs all others, no-one stands where He trod.
His balanced justice levels down the proud.
You exercised rightful judgment before
In Jacob and You led Your chosen priests
Moses and Aaron, also Samuel, who called.
They kept and taught those testimonies Your
Wisdom gave them and celebrated those feasts
Marking special events in giving the Law.
When their inventions got the upper hand
You punished sin and made them understand.

100. Jubilate Deo.

O be joyful in the Lord all you lands:
With cheerful hearts serve the Lord, add a spring
To your step as you whistle a happy tune.
Have no doubt that the Lord is God: fortune
Cannot deny it. From the beginning
We are the sheep of His pasture. His hands
Made us not we ourselves. In Him is life
So go your way thankfully citywards:
Sing praises as loud as ardor affords
In the courts of His house, both man and wife.
For He is gracious, speak of His name
As good and merciful; so spread His fame.
His truth endures throughout generations:
His justice established amongst the nations.

101.

I include Your mercy in my ballad
And sing of Your judgment. My demeanor
Shall be acceptable to invite You home
If You improve my understanding. Come,
Teach me. I will mark my behavior
And not put my hand to things that are bad.
My sole aim is to avoid falling short
Since I despise sin and cleave to Your rule.
I'll put an end to the slandering fool,
I've no time for the haughty and their sort.
I look for the faithful to share our school
Of thought for godly service as all ought.
To the deceitful no door will open
For I'll root out the wicked and rotten.

102.

Hear my entreaties Lord. Don't turn away.
I am totally downcast and have noted
How my enemies revile me and swear
To do me down while I waste away. Bear
With me for You've cast me aside. I've quoted
You endure continuing in one stay.
But come, pity Sion[10]: her stones now lie
In the dust: see how her people are subdued.
When You restore Sion You will reveal
Your glory and the heathen'll know You deal
With justice. Look down from on high how crude
Is our treatment and we fear we shall die.
Death is inevitable while You endure:
But our descendants continue we're sure.

---

10. Sion often identified with Jerusalem = Place of Peace.

103. A Suitable Psalm To Include At A Funeral Service.

Praise the Lord with my whole being: Forget
Not all His benefits. Infirmities
He heals and forgives sin. He spares our lives
From destruction, the penitent survives.
Since Moses He's shown mercy, His realities
Are judgment and justice in His hands yet.
His verdict is better than we deserve
His mercy extends as heaven is high:
He sets our sins as far as the East
Is from the West though from Him we swerve.
We are dust we flourish no more than die
Like wild flowers. His provision a feast
While His goodness endures forever the same.
Respond with praise and speak good of His name.

104. Consider The Environment, The Waters.

Glorious light radiates round Your garments.
You control the waters of the deep
And command the valleys that rivers keep.
Your hand quenches the thirst of beasts, prevents
Drought from shriveling our vineyards and fields.
You provide food for fish so the sea yields.
From moisture trees draw strength wherein birds nest.
You appoint seasons, the sun and moon to rest.
When You breathe life into fauna it thrives,
Flora and Biodiversity reflect
Your Majesty but sadly we detect
It fares badly once Mankind arrives.
You hide Your face, all fades, we can't rejoice:
Displeasing the Lord stifles a cheerful voice.

Ancient shrine to Pan at Banias (Dan) incorporated into Caesarea Philippi and the gate to Hades in the old myths. 1974.

105.

Give thanks to the Lord and extol His name.
Tell of His works and the marvelous things
He has done; of His covenant honored
Throughout generations since Abraham
And Jacob's promised inheritance.
Moses opposed Pharaoh's obdurate stance,
He reproved Egypt whose word was a sham
Calling down the disastrous plagues God poured.
Visit us with Your salvation which brings
Joy like when our forefathers knew Your fame.
Remember me. You favored them, supplied
Their needs. We sin like them when they denied
You in the wilderness. You forgave their apostasy
Keeping true to Your covenant with constancy.

106. This Adds The Conclusion Of How Their Tempting God Unfolded:

We have sinned like our fathers who ignored
Your sustaining them in the wilderness:
First they believed then forgot when challenged.
The earth opened and Dathan was swallowed:
Fire consumed their ring leaders who worshiped
The golden calf,[11] until Moses interceded.
Again they ignored God eating offerings
To others' gods. Their murmuring returned.
Aaron failed. Moses with indignation burned.
They failed to cleanse the land they conquered
Removing temptation and idols worshiped,
Sacrificing children. Each time they lapsed
God forgave and remembered His covenant.
Let the people say Amen, God is constant.

---

11. To represent the Canaanite god El, symbol of strength, worship of which was a constant fall-back in the days after Solomon.

107.[12]

When they cried to the Lord in their distress
He delivered them: would that people praise Him,
Declaring His wonders, how the hungry
Soul is fed full. When they fell He heard their cry.
Those who conduct business on waters grim,
And experience the deep sea's fastness,
Encounter storm and tumultuous waves.
Frightened they cry to the Lord who saves
Bidding the storm to cease. Then they're happy
Brought unto the haven where they would be.
Declare His wonders. Praise the Lord's goodness.
He commands waters, floods the wilderness
That the hungry may sow crops, the fields yield.
The righteous consider He's their shield.

---

12. Compare the accounts of Jesus stilling the storm and how the waters of baptism offer a haven in life (John 6:16–21).

108.

My heart is ready to praise God, employing
The best skills I have. My thanks shall lead people.
Your mercy and truth are boundless as the sky.
Let Your glory enfold the earth, and why?
That those You love, gathered in Your temple,
May be delivered. You rejoice by toying
With our neighboring adversaries
And bending them to Your service.
They're Your possessions and they pay Your price.
We need You, O Lord, to throw off their ties.
Do not forsake us. Won't You accompany
Our soldiers? Against the enemy
Neighboring states are a vain alliance
When we know that God is our reliance.

Another Look At 108. Cryptic! Expanding On Moab Is My Washpot, Since Every Name Has A Meaning.[13]

When Israel occupied Canaan's coast
Joshua parceled Philistia
To the twelve tribes by lot. Migration
Gave way to triumph by God's direction.
Foremost Judah became His law giver,
Well fortified red Edom's fall His boast.
Might those picking up the cast-off shoe
Claim surplus Edom for an inheritance?
Rocky Gilead came into possession,
The shoulder of Sichem saw division,
His Manasses forgot allegiance,
Daughters' booths in Succoth were ended too.
Ephraim's doubly fruitful strength of my head
Saw Moab, water of a father, cleansed.

13. Moab = Water of a Father; Philistia = migration; Judah = praise; Edom = red; Giliad = rocky, strong; Sichem = ridge, shoulder; Manasseh = causing forgetfulness; Succoth = booths; Ephraim = doubly fruitful.

109.

Don't hold Your tongue, God. I praise You. Heathen
Mouths full of deceit decry me: despite
My goodwill their response is contrary.
My good is not rewarded: a quandary
I fail to understand. I will incite
You to turn their lives into a burden:
Cut their lives short, may they be condemned
By their own words and their children orphaned,
Begging their bread. May their wealth be consumed
By loan sharks, their labor rejected and spoiled.
Destroy their inheritance, their mothers blamed,
Their names blotted out. My fasting they mocked.
Let those who curse me be confounded and shamed
Since my redeemer in my praise is named.

110.

The Lord said to my Lord: Sit on My right
Till I put your enemies in subjection.
The Lord will strengthen your ruling arm
From Zion and shield you from any harm.
Then people in worship from every section
Will bring their freewill offerings: your light
Has revealed a new dawn for them. The Lord
Will not go back on His Word. Priest you are
Forever like Melchisedech[14] who brings
Bread and wine as offerings. Hostile kings,
With the Lord on your right hand, should beware
His wrath. He will judge the heathen, accord
Justice and subjugate opposition.
He'll drink safely with no hesitation.[15]

---

14. Melchisedech = My King is Righteous. Genesis 14:17–20; Hebrews 5:5–10; 7:1–3.

15. See Judges 7:4–8. Gideon chose ones drinking safely and remaining alert.

111. The Fear Of The Lord Is The Beginning Of Wisdom (Psalm 112:1; Proverbs 9:10.)

I'll give thanks to the Lord wholeheartedly
In private and in public: His great works
Are much admired and to all give pleasure.
His work is worthy of note: the treasure
Is His righteousness. He never shirks
His responsibilities: deadly
Is His wrath but His mercy endures.
He feeds the fearful, is ever mindful
Of His covenant displaying His power
To His people while the heathen cower
Forfeiting their fatherland. He's graceful,
The epitome of truth. He ensures
His commandments usher in His kingdom:
Fear of the Lord is the start of Wisdom.

112.

Blessed is the person who fears the Lord
Taking delight in His ten commandments.
Successfully shall his successors keep
That family going and God shall heap
His rewards on the faithful whose comments
Will light the lives of others and afford
Them true guidance and generosity.
Notable for their discretion they will be
Remembered for all their righteousness.
Established they will exercise kindness
To the unfortunate but no pity
In the face of any hostility.
All the ungodly faced with such honor
Will be disappointed and find no succor.

113.

Praise the Lord who reverses misfortune
And comes to the rescue of the importune.
Daily is His name blessed now and always,
Way up high above all His glory stays.
Who is like the Lord God on high who deigns
To be humble and behold any who reigns
On earth below and mark all their doings?
It is the Lord who gets a grip of things.
Out of the dust He takes the simple and lifts
The poor from the mire: society shifts
When lesser are sat with the great and good
And He orders wellbeing as He should.
The childless woman at His direction
Will be a joyful mother of perfection.

114.

When the Israelites left Egypt and ceased
To be aliens in a foreign land
Judah became their sanctuary
And Israel their given realm. Red Sea
Waters retreated, at Jordan God's own hand
Divided the river: conquest increased.
The mountains danced in awesome attendance
As if they skipped and likewise hills gamboled
Like lambs. What must have caused the sea to flee,
And Jordan's waters to part? What spooked hills
And mountains to leap like sheep? The Lord fills
The earth with His presence and majesty
So tremble before Him whose might has enrolled
The rocks into His service to provide
Water to sustain life from deep inside.

115.

May You, Lord, take praise. Not from us, from You
Springs truth: we benefit from Your mercy.
Well may the heathen ask, Where's your God then?
He's in heaven doing what pleases hissen.[16*]
As for their gods they're good for nothing, see.
For all their silver and gold, shining new,
They are but the work of men and artists.
They have mouths but canna speak nor utter.
They've eyes but canna see, no lids flutter.
They've ears but canna hear, deafness exists.
They've noses but canna smell; or that, phew!
They've hands but canna hold corn and strew.
They've feet but canna walk a step when shod.
Who makes 'em are dead like 'em. Our help's God.

---

16. A Yorkshire expression for himself.

116. The Cup Of Judgment In Psalm 75 Becomes The Cup Of Salvation.

I'm pleased the Lord heard my prayer, therefore
I shall address Him always all my days.
I felt like death, as if drawn down to Hell:
When so troubled I beseeched the Lord to quell
My anxiety for deliverance pays:
The Lord is gracious, we praise Him more.
He preserves the simple: when in misery
He helped me, He exercises mercy.
I will walk before Him 'mongst the living.
How can I reward the Lord's benefits?
I will receive the cup of salvation.
I'll speak publicly, avoid temptation;
Having freedom I'll serve Him as befits.
I'll offer Him sacrifices of thanksgiving.

117.

I choose my words carefully. I intend
To number my high regard for Your law
Letter by letter through the alphabet
Enumerating highlights and my debt
To Your influence that will endure
For ever that even heathen will bend
To the discipline of Your yoke on us.
We so enjoy Your merciful kindness
That it demands our thanks and praise.
Come you unbelievers, join us to raise
Hymns of appreciation to witness
To God's truth that you really need to suss.
What could be easier than to worship
The gentle God of grace so let our songs rip!

118.

The Lord is gracious so give thanks whose
Mercy endures forever. When in trouble
I call on Him: what man can be afraid
With the Lord alongside because no aid
Is forthcoming from fellow men. Double
Is their oppression like bees but I choose
To place my trust in God for salvation
And enter His gates to offer thanksgiving
For deliverance. It appears the stone
The builders refused is the foundation:
It's marvelous witnessing the Lord's doing.
It's the Lord's day rejoice, for sin atone.
Blessed is he that comes in the Lord's name!
Light enters the world to disperse our shame.

119.

Through Adoration I seek Your Blessing.
I give Careful Dedication to assessing
Your Education in study Finding
Your Glory is Heaven's Illustration.
Justified I Keep Your Law and Mercy
Is Your reward. To Your Holy Name
I Open my heart in Praise Quietening
My soul. Revealed in Scripture I find Truth.
Your Word is wisdom and Understanding.
I am Vindicated my steps following
The paths of Your Way. All eXpectation
Is fulfilled Yearning for Your presence:
Indeed it would seem that every dream
Is Zion's reality that You redeem.[17]

---

17. In the spirit of Psalm where each section begins with each letter of the Hebrew alphabet in turn I have made a play on A-Z in this summary.

A Summary Of Psalm 119

To study Your Word is my pleasure;
Your directions dictate my leisure.
Thus my path in life is straight and narrow
Brim full with joy, quite distant from sorrow.
The enemy within You calm and tame:
My only watchword is Your holy name.
My delight is in Your statutes: I live
To represent You to others so give
Me understanding to explain Your law
That others recognise righteousness
And learn what distances us is selfishness.
Without Your guidance we're stray sheep. Poor
Are those who forget You: once left behind
To Your presence a closed door they will find.

120.

The Lord heard when in trouble I called on Him
To deliver my soul from lies and slander.
What rewards can satisfy those speaking
Ill if not a pricking and gentle roasting.
What a constraint when those who philander
Are my neighbors: also I am appalled
Living amongst those who are powerful
Who deny me peace and tranquility
Even though they surround me. If I mention
Peace I am shouted down for their intention
Is to go out to battle, ignore quality
Of life supposing their god's wonderful.
Woe is me if the Lord lends no support
Else placed as I am my life will be short.

121. Most Suitable For A Funeral.

I shall look up the hills anticipating
My help from God Himself descending
Since He is that source, the very maker
Of heaven and earth, the instigator
Of security that when defending
My pitch I stand firm. The Lord is waiting
With sleepless watch guarding Israel.
The Lord's your keeper and ready defense.
So even the sun won't burn you by day
Nor the moon at night. He keeps at bay
All evil ensuring preservation hence
Your soul remains as safe as you can tell.
The Lord guards all you do, your enterings
And exitings and whatever life brings.

122. I Was Glad When They Said Unto Me We Will Go Into The House Of The Lord.

My heart leapt for joy when they said, "We'll go
Into the Lord's house." In Jerusalem
Shall we stand which is built as a city
Offering concord, enjoying harmony.
There the Lord's chosen ascend, each stem
Of those tribes from patriarchal stock, to
Bear witness to God and their faith affirm
With thanks. King David's throne is there, the seat
Of judgment. For Jerusalem's[18] peace pray,
Her well-being and prosperity. May
In turn those who care for her welfare meet
Rewards for themselves in the long term.
For the benefit of family and those to hand,
Neighbors, to wish Your good I understand.

---

18. Jerusalem = Place of Peace.

123.

I look up to God who above us dwells.
I look as a servant'll anticipate
His master's hand or the eyes of her maid
Look on her mistress how to be obeyed.
Similarly upon God I will wait
Expectant His mercy evil repels.
Certainly we seek Your mercy O Lord
For we are rejected and scorned
For no obvious reasons but belief
In Your name and saving grace. No relief
Comes but through You. Our critics should be warned
The other sides of such coin afford
The wealth of our reproof for their treasure
And as much disdain as the proud measure.

124.

Without the Lord on our side Israel
Can say, yes and repeat, without the Lord
On our side those who rose up against us
Would have swallowed us up since they cuss
For reasons known just to them and reward
Us for causing their displeasure with well
Aimed hostility and opposition.
It's like we were overwhelmed by rising
Waters and we were near drowned by the stream
Losing our very soul. The proud might deem
In their own murky depths that we're losing
Our soul, but praise the Lord's intervention
Who prevented our being their prey breaking
Their snare: we escaped like a bird on the wing.

The foothills of Hermon. A knocked-out Syrian T-54 from the Six Day War. 1974.

125.

All putting trust in the Lord shall be stable
As Mount Sion which cannot be removed,
Since it will stand forever. As hills stand
Round Jerusalem so does the Lord stand
Round His people with stability proved
From time immemorial. None is able
Among the ungodly ranks to intrude
On the righteous when God prevents
The latter from turning to wickedness.
Uphold those who pursue righteousness,
O Lord, and steer clear of pagan events.
Those who return to their old ways and lewd
Worship shall be marched out with the evil
By the Lord but peace is Israel's fill.

126.

When the Lord reversed Sion's captivity
And freed her people then life seemed a dream.
We were laughing and filled with happiness;
We spread the good news that reality
Had returned and the heathen remarked, "They seem
To have great things done by their Lord's kindness."
For certainly the Lord has done great things
And jubilation through the city rings.
Release us, Lord, freedom's flow to enjoy.
Those who sow tearfully will reap in joy.
Even the person who walks weeping and
Takes good seed along with him sown by hand
Without doubt shall return as harvest matures
Bearing sheaves from the ripe crops God ensures.

127. "Nisi Dominus Frustra" Read The Lintel Of Our Yorkshire Vicarage.

Unless the Lord builds the house the builders
Labor in vain. Unless the Lord keep
The city duty sentries wake in vain.
Those who chase about all day for no gain,
Rising early and retiring late heap
Cares on their heads while life bewilders.
The Lord grants His beloved peaceful sleep.
Children are a gift in life and the fruit
Of joyful union; a heritage
From the Lord indicates great advantage.
A quiver full, so to speak, will contribute
To a man's happiness as arrows keep
His standing at the gate with the sentries
When confronted by hordes of enemies.

128.

The fear of the Lord leads to blessedness,
Especially for any who walk
The way that the Lord would have them follow.
All shall be well and joy your status quo.
You shall eat the fruit of your labors. Talk,
Since your family shall so folk impress,
Will center on your wife's fecundity:
She shall be as fruitful as vines adorn
The wall of your house. Your children around
Your table shall be to your credit sound
And lasting as an olive grove. Born
To be blessed and enjoy prosperity
Is anyone who respects the Lord. More
Generations have peace that God adore.

129. They Shall Not Benefit From The Blessing "The Lord Prosper You."

Often have I had to bear arms since my
Youth, may Israel say, though our armies
Prevented our enemies prevailing.
Nevertheless we suffered torturing
When they ploughed furrows despite our cries
Across our backs. However those who defy
The Lord are confounded; He springs the traps
And upsets the wiles of those wishing evil
Intent on Sion. After the sun's sucked
Moisture from rooftop grass before it's plucked
By the farmer so the Lord will strike still
Leaving nothing for the mower, just gaps
For those collecting sheaves. None will offer
Greetings nor passers-by blessings proffer.

130.

From the depths of despair I have called You:
Hear me, my Lord. Listen as carefully
As You can and consider my complaint.
If You want to be wayward, leave me faint,
And fail to notice what's been done wrongly.
Who can survive or tolerate that too?
You're the seat of mercy delivering
Impartial justice so all shall fear
You and respect Your name. My soul awaits
The Lord to whom I look up and who hates
Those who disregard Him. His word I hear
And trust. My soul takes refuge each morning
With the Lord. Israel trust His mercy
For there on redemption you can rely.

131.

I am not above myself, neither proud
Nor haughty; I am not involved in things
Or affairs beyond me. I have no guile.
I restrain myself, keep a low profile,
So I refrain from empty ponderings
And expressing opinions out loud.
I maintain a stillness like a weaned child
No longer needing my mother's breast
But confident of like security
Now that I find trust in the Lord's pity.
Thus sated peacefully do I take my rest.
Israel trust the Lord who's never riled.
Give God glory, Father, Son, Spirit all three
Ever and always as One They shall be.

132.

Lord, remember David's vow in his troubles
That he wouldn't rest until he found a place
For Your house, a place to worship and keep
Vigil, forsaking his own chapel, and sleep
In his own bed. I will find the right space
Though I rack my brains and my effort doubles.
We've heard rumors and made visits and found
Templates for the Lord's resting place and ark.
Set Yourself there, let saints sing joyfully,
Your priests minister, accept dutifully
Your Anointed as You promised, and mark
The loyalty of his children now bound
To keep Your lessons and laws. They will lead
Your chosen Sion whom You bless and feed.

133. Unity.

What a wonderful world it is when folk
Live like brothers in unity! A sight
To enjoy and celebrate! An example
To others that here is a chance to sample
Peace and security, a worthwhile light
To better days. There's no need for the woke!
Unity's valuable like a symbol sure
Of precious ointment over the head,
Even like that which ran down Aaron's beard
And clothing, or as dew before it cleared
On Mount Hermon and on Sion instead.
There the Lord promised life for evermore.
There the Lord promised to bless unity
Amongst men and long life in the city.

Mount Hermon from the walls of Banias. 1974.

134.

Come, gather together all you servants
Of the Lord and give Him your heartfelt praise
As is His due. You, too, that keep compline
And a night vigil in His house incline
Your worship to be uplifting and raise
Your voices in song along His courts. Savants
Of music lead the tune! Lift up your hands
In the sanctuary: adoration
And praise are expected to be forthcoming
From you and with your instruments strumming.
(Your worship is basic recognition.)
Praise the Lord, maker of heavens, the lands
Of the earth and the seas, who, ever same,
His blessing from holy Sion will proclaim.

135.

Praise the Lord all you servants of the Lord.
All standing in the Lord's courts acknowledge
His graciousness with thanks. Why? He opted
To select Jacob and also adopted
Israel, since it pleased Him to pledge
His love like He rules the elements. Applaud
His wonders in Egypt, His slaughtered kings of old
To award His chosen their lands.[19] His name
Became an enduring memorial;
His gracious rule is imperial.
Heathen gods enjoy no lasting fame:
They're men's handiwork in silver and gold,
Whose faculties don't respond any more
Nor answer prayers of those stood before.

    19. Psalms 135 and 136. It is worth noting names of the foreign kings and lands mentioned since they fill out the picture of the fruitful land that Israel is still today and the power of those they overcame: Amorites = mountaineers (Canaan is also called Mount of the Amorites); Sihon = bold; Og = giant (Goliath type); Bashan = fruitful.

136. His Mercy Endures For Ever.

Give thanks to the gracious Lord; number
His wonders for His mercy endures.
His excellent wisdom made creation:
Heavens and earth, seas and light, the station
Of the sun, moon and stars. Thus He ensures
The world's regulation when in slumber
Or activity. His mighty action
Delivered Israel, slaves in Egypt,
When through the divided Red Sea they slipt
Leaving Pharoah's armies to destruction.
He led them through the wilderness giving
Into their hands enemies and their lands[20]
Which became our heritage that still stands
For which we offer God our thanksgiving.

20. What's in a name to describe those lands? Hivites = villagers; Jebusites = sons of Jebus; Hittites = people of Heth in the mountains; Perizzites = hill country tribe; Ephraim = doubly fruitful; Amorites = mountaineers; Girgashite = tribe long settled in Canaan.

137.

We sat by the waters of Babylon
And wept when we remembered our old city
Of Sion, and hung our harps in the trees.
Our captors taunted us to sing melodies
Of our homeland showing us no pity.
Can we sing the Lord's songs looking upon
A strange land when we are full of sadness?
May I never forget our Jerusalem
Or I would lose my ingenuity.
May I be dumb in perpetuity
If I cannot remember in my mirth
That gem of a place and land of my birth.
(Remember Edomites who you condemn:
Destroy their children in the wilderness.)

138.

I shall thank God always with my whole heart:
I shall draw near Your holy places to praise
Your loving kindness and truth, above all
For Your blessed Word who answers our call.
Thereby You endue me with strength and raise
My soul. May all earthly kings play their part
On hearing Your words in singing of Your ways
And proclaiming the story of Your glory.
While the Lord is high He respects the low
And can see the proud coming with their show.
When I find myself in trouble victory
Comes my way from the Lord, an assured phase
Of His loving kindness. His mercy endures.
Don't despise Your handiwork, Lord, that cures.

139.

You, Lord, know me inside out! When I sit
Down or get up to stand You know. In fact
You know my thoughts even before I do.
You're where I walk or talk, by my bed too.
You made me: it's hard to grasp. No contact
With Your Spirit is impossible. I can't flit
From You in Your every dimension
Nor escape Your own hand in creation.
Darkness or night with You is clear as day.
Controlled from my birth You have kept Your say:
Indeed I find Your guidance precious
And to count Your counsel too numerous.
Keep those who hate You away from me, please,
And know my loyal thoughts shall never cease.

140.

Deliver me, Lord, from the evil and
Keep me from the wicked's mischief: slander
And strife are his sharp methods: his vain pride
Undermines my doings, takes me for a ride.
Hear my prayers, Lord, give strength, don't pander
To the desires of the ungodly band.
(May those who surround me fall victim
To their curses and roast in their own pot.)
No-one full of bombast and tommyrot
Shall prosper: evil shall stalk and tumble him.
I'm certain the Lord will avenge the poor
And He'll maintain the cause of the helpless.
The righteous shall offer thankfulness
And to the just You shall open Your door.

141.

Consider my voice when on You I call:
Accept my prayer scented like incense waft.
I raise hands as an evening sacrifice.
Watch what I say, nothing at any price
Must come between us. I will not go soft
Eating such offerings as may please all
The ungodly occupied in their works.
I'd rather the righteous cut me down!
Don't let them cover me with fragrant spices,
Because I will pray against their practices.
(May their judges be condemned and overthrown
And hear me speak the truth where now death lurks.)
I look up to You, Lord, and put my trust.
Get caught in their own traps the wicked must!

142.

I poured out my troubles to the Lord: I cried
Out in making my requests when depressed.
You know how fully in Your Word I'm wrapped
But my adversaries had booby trapped
My path and in my plight no one addressed
Themselves to my help knowing my foes lied.
I said to the Lord, "You're my only hope
And my lot this side of the grave." Please hear
Me for I am very disconsolate.
They're so strong I need you to liberate
Me from my oppressors who cause my fear.
It's their imprisonment that makes me mope
So deliver me, then my thanks I'll give
And with righteous company I'll live.

143.

Hear my prayer, Lord, consider my needs.
Don't judge Your servant since no-one living
Can be justified before You. My foes
Oppress me and are the source of my woes.
I remember old times and Your giving
Light to my paths so on You my soul feeds
When fainting. Just look at me, else I die.
Let me awake to Your loving kindness.
Teach me the way to be, answer my trust
For You are my refuge from those who lust
For my downfall. Land of righteousness
Be my destination where no troubles lie.
Keep me alive for the sake of Your name
Destroying those who won't serve You the same.

144.

The blessed Lord strengthens me, my sure defense.
He taught the art of war, engendered trust.
What is man, Lord, that You respect him so
Or with such a high opinion You go
To any lengths for a mere mortal? Must
You have time for those whose stuff is less dense
Than a shadow? Descend and deliver
Me from strangers whose talk is vanity.
Then I will sing songs of deliverance
As was David from the sword's fateful chance.
On our sons and daughters show Your pity
That they prosper and shine. You're the giver
Of plenty and freedom; there's no complaint.
With such a great God who could ever faint?

145.

I will venerate the Lord and always
Praise His name expansively.
I will offer my grateful thanks daily
To our great God, ever worthy of praise.
Generation to generation shall raise
Awareness of His power, echoed too
By men from their own experience who
Sing of His righteousness—a mere phrase
In memorial of His abundant love.
The Lord in His gracious goodness is
Long suffering however wayward man is!
The works of the Lord are His praise above
All we utter. He opens His hand to feed
All life and in answer meet every need.

146. Matthew 25:31-46 (Called The Judgment).

While I have breath praise the Lord, O my soul.
Don't place your trust in princes, nor mere men,
For you'll find no help there. When men perish
They return to dust and their thoughts finish.
Our blessings lie in a live God, no wooden
Image, whose continuity of the whole
Line of our Patriarchs ensures our help.
He formed creation and keeps His promises.
He helps the wronged, feeds the hungry,
Releases the captive, makes the blind to see,
Raises the fallen, steps into our crises,
Cares for strangers, orphans, the widow's whelp.
He turns the ungodly's ways upside down,
For generations our King of renown.

147.

It brings joy to the heart to offer thanks
And praise to the Lord who has established
Jerusalem and scoops up the outcast.
He heals the broken-hearted and sick. Past
Number are the stars but named as He wished
In His infinite wisdom. Heathen ranks
He brings down but makes the meek stand upright.
He waters the earth, grass and herbs flourish
So man and beast feed, even ravens do.
He secures Sion[21], her children within too.
Frost, ice and snow obey His every wish:
Peace and prosperity become birthright.
What other nation enjoys such attention?
Of His laws the heathen make no mention.

---

21. For Sion understand Jerusalem = Place of Peace.

SW corner of Temple Mount and Al-Aqsa mosque above old gate and washing area. Priests' houses would have been in the foreground. 1974.

148. Praise Indeed!

Let all creation praise the Lord of might,
His angels and all the hosts in the height,
Sun, moon, the canopy of stars, and light.
The waters above and below He made
With a Word and set each in position.
He interlocks fast His composition
Bringing air and elements to fruition.
All gave Him due honor as they obeyed.
On earth He called forth life, trees in their kind,
Beasts, birds, and all sorts that move He refined,
Products of His Spirit and creative mind.
Let Humanity praise His worthy name,
His love and excellent Wisdom proclaim.

149. A Church's Response.

Sing a new hymn to the Lord. The gathered
Church, servant saints, raise a chorus of praise.
Let Israel rejoice in His being,
Sion's children in the King they're seeing.
May they dance plucking their harps all their days
With tambourines, all whom the Lord fathered.
You are His pleasure. He helps the meek.
Let all the Lord's saints express His glory,
Sleep soundly, and proclaim loud His story:
To the heathen may they bring correction,
'Gainst ignoble rulers offer protection,
And foster any whom the Lord would seek.
Thus God's faithful are agents of restraint:
In freedom there's honor for every saint.

150.

Come, praise the Lord with everything you've got:
Whatever your instruments play the lot!
Praise His holiness, praise His seat of power,
Praise Him for all He does, with a shower
Of anthems exalt His greatness. The sound
Of trumpets herald His fame. All around
Strings of lutes and harps resound all can dance.
Include tunes on the pipe; don't leave to chance
Your accompaniment with percussion,
Rather let the cymbals join the session.
Let every thing that has breath sing praise
Of the Lord and pyramids of song raise.
Give God glory, Father, Son, Spirit, all three:
Ever and always as One They shall be.

Hezekiah's or the Siloam Tunnel, Jerusalem. Water is ever a theme in the psalms but guarding the water supply was all-important as the well was without the city walls. 2 Chronicles 32:30. 2 Kings 20:20. 750 feet long, hewn by men from both ends at the same time to give access to the Gihon spring (where Solomon had been anointed) when the city was fortified against Sennacharib. 1988.

Entrance to Hezekiah's Tunnel from city. 1988.

SECTION 2.

And Other Matters Spiritual
In the Light of Faith

Spirit of Geology

Can we be sure of firm foundations?
What of Noah's flood by inundations?
Even our island's bedrock moved round
The globe from Australasia sound
To mysterious Loch Ness's rugged
Northern flank pushed not tugged
By forces revealed through geology
That number this earth's chronology
As millennia galore by the score
That God counts but a day of yore.
So fundamentalists must retune
To listen to this world's ancient rune
Marking nature's course and early ages
As God made the world by goodly stages.

Myths, Cult and Practice

What myths become faith's background
Shaping our Christian story from cult?
Are descriptions adjusted when found
From ancient explanations, difficult
To paint, to scenes in turn to capture
Struggling imaginations as people lagged?
Who was St. George: soldier sure,
Perseus personified, now flagged?
Did the dragon personify evilness?
Does Mariology absorb former worship sessions
Of Ceres Mother Earth's fruitfulness?
These Greek to Roman to Christian progressions
Were rewritten by the faithful's first impressions
As Wisdom reorientated early expressions.

Memorials.

Memorials tell a story
From a family point of view
Either individual glory
Or life with a more tragic hue.
Wives who die in childbirth
Or of husbands killed in war;
Sometimes their lives have hints of mirth,
Or of dead children by the score.
Each and every memory
Carved on church walls or graveyard stones
Tells us we aren't judge or jury
Of those whose meaning now God owns.
All played a part bringing us to be
Marking their own posterity.

God in the Garden.

Of Adam "Where are you?" asked God at the fall,
Portrayed by the Son as a Prodigal cheat.
As parents summon their children with a call
From play in the garden to wash and to eat
We will hear God speak in His still small voice.
When we know it is ourselves whom God seeks
Silence is broken, to listen our choice.
(He clothed Adam before his exit with breeks!)
That awareness of a parental God minding
Looking out for us has more coverage
In the Bible than our feeble efforts at finding
Him ourselves and trying to engage.
He remains at the heart of resurrection
That mirrors our lives needing reconciliation.

Integrity, 1 Peter: Lambeth 2022.

To build up the faith requires integrity
As Peter would emphasize with pity
For those distracted by the world and flesh.
We need Wisdom our world to refresh
For nothing save God's love is fixed or static
Seeking us out and drawing us on. Erratic,
The Anglican Communion is a legacy
Of past empire now outdated at least
In need of restoring a global efficacy
Of values, truth, and cures as the yeast
To leaven the lump the world has become.
Man's response to the Word is far too numb;
With focus on the Me what hope for us all
Unless all Christians reverse a new Fall?

Can AI Have a Soul?

If you develop a system to think
It will depend on the logic equipping
Its algorithms to get up and starting:
That cannot be soul imparting.
Many folk think and reason without stripping
Away evidence of a soul. Do we shrink
Or grow in Spirit through life lived for others?
Robots are made to care and serve with inbuilt
Routine but not anticipate as a loving spouse
Or caring neighbor calling at the house.
Can AI possibly feel guilt?
Or recognise a soul in others?
Surely how the program is applied
Dictates parameters and soul denied.

The Funeral of HRH Queen Elizabeth II.

Carried with dignity and respect
Horses and children at the walk,
Placed on a catafalque to lie in state.
The mourning world pass to reflect,
The media record and recollect.
A new order begins to percolate.
Officials observe due ceremony, much talk
About such events. Royal occasions
Take place with measured pace
Rehearsed long since past. Recognition
Due to a long reign's persuasions
Has not missed a generation.
Gracious service remembered
At services in turn eulogies heard.

Hospitality. (Stranger at Your Manger.)

Martha provided so the Lord did sup;
Debatable whether Mary washed up!
All are destined to their chosen path.
Some will grumble while others will laugh.
Round the table all are equal to share the same
Regardless of status including the lame.
There's always abundance in our Lord's name,
More so the bread whose substance we acclaim.
Hospitality demands all set aside
Differences and security provide.
Whatever is cooked and the table is set
Be sure those gathered around are well met.
May the cup they share be a great blessing
Not judgment despite circumstances pressing.

Further to Fr Mykhailo Dymyd's Heartfelt Reflection on "Therapy at War. How Can We Heal the Heart of Conflict?" Ukraine.

The loss of a close loved one costs and leads
To transformation through sacrifice
When evil is encountered. The mystery
In the context of Communion is victory
Of the Spirit. Experience must suffice
To bridge the chasm where discussion feeds
Into stories. Wisdom springs from reflection,
Conclusion emerges from consideration.
Sacrifice is a hard consecration.
Let the wider Church promote reconciliation
Through symbolic ritual. Humiliation
Leaves stigma, fueling substitution
In transgenerational discord,
Not resulting in resolution's reward.

Memory I.

Memory collective and individual
Plays its part preserving particular stories
In museum, poetry, and debate, to fuel
Dialogue, locate the plus and minus, glories
And losses of time past to build time future
In time present, ever always in motion.
Can paperless memory the truth ensure?
Can art rather than myth foster some notion
Of reconciliation to engender peace?
Objects of the times mutate as symbols of what must
Be heard, celebrated, or become a hard lesson;
Can they be shared in Church or teach posterity?
What decisions stoke forgiveness or dissent?
Not forgotten is forgiveness received with assent?

Memory II.

Memory prompts a voice, alerts an ear,
Holding a story for posterity to hear.
When shared does she stir diversity
Or consent? Can we trust her integrity
To find reconciliation's common ground
Rather than keep alive an open wound?
Leaving narrative for dialogue progresses
Honesty and each mistakes confesses.
Memory starts paperless; from what is stored
Can we build not burden but a record
Where former sides agree to differ, find
Understanding and trust that call to mind
Past events in a perspective to forgive?
Then build mutual welfare and so live.

Memory III.

We are given memory to use or reject
By which accepted faith becomes the object
To level and understand our experiences,
A revealed guide not from the sciences.
There is collected memory in prayer from fact
And collective memory given by contract.
"In thy light may we see light," the psalmist said
That from God's angle truth is read.
"Do this in memory of me"; Jesus instead
Gave a rule that mastered dissent putting a view
And replacing the Old Testament with the New.
For those prepared to move on His symbol was bread.
It's a memory that stands and by which some fall:
True peace follows when memorial serves all.

Spain. After 1482 Alhambra's Changing Ownership.

Sunlight strikes Alhambra's red-walled towers,
Seat of changing Sultans' powers;
A place of garden walks and leafy bowers.
Impregnable on watered spur it stands
Above a secured city and commands
The Pomegranate province. Comfort demands
The airy rooms catch a cooling breeze
So kings and queens could take their ease.
Plaster stucco, Cuban wood, and tiled frieze
Decorate all well written walls inside—
"There is no God but God"—warnings provide
Where justice was served till Boabdil sighed.
Departing French accelerated decay
Less what was soldier-saved you see today.

Alhambra Upper Private Palace Gardens, Granada, Spain. 2023.

Cultural Diplomacy. Revealing the Soul of Nations.

Exchange culture to know each other more,
Shared soul through arts, faith and each tradition.
Creative freedom fosters condition
Where parties engage to exchange their store
Of experience and outlook expressed
In painting, sculpture, song and story,
Open discussion, dance and history,
Identity through heritage impressed.
Exhibitions through the curator's eyes
Become narrative to open debate
Seeking that common ground where each relate
To find comparisons. Suspicion dies:
The unfamiliar is presented whole
Through the familiar to bare the soul.

Advent.

The choir sang a pyramid of praise
As chant built upon chant, Sarum Rite,
While darkness was overcome with candle light
Increasing down nave stations with each phase.
Opening cantor with antiphonal
Chant starts the procession before
Responsorial singers around the floor
And gallery add their parts. Modal
'O' s open as Wisdom, Key, Root, Dayspring
Name Christ echoing anticipation
For His coming and the preparation
Which expectant hearts for Emmanuel sing.
Salisbury's plain glass enclose anthems
Sourcing where true spirituality stems.

Advent Scene.

Rows of Advent candles Eastwards point their light
Past standard raised clusters to a focal point
Where the colored stained sanctuary glass
Is back lit. Anthems and hymns as choirs pass
Surround the scene with a volume, now joint
Now antiphonal, of song. More delight
From a galleried group of girls as one voice
Uphold the congregation to rejoice
With son et lumière within nave's height
And remember Emmanuel this night.
Beyond the gray shadows where the arrow
Of candlelight extends looms the East window
A block of primary colors without detail
Like the rainbow signaled Noah floods would fail.

God Displaced. Oxford Martin Discussion on Strongmen in Politics with Lord Patten, Gideon Rachman & Margaret MacMillan. 28/11/22.

Strongmen stand after winning to control all
Limiting support save from those in thrall
Dependent on dancing the autocrat's tune.
Meanwhile the world is hostage to fortune
Unless vanity causes a mighty fall.
Democracy eroded, "It's fake" they call.
Media promotes personality cult
Confronting enemies of their making
Claiming to speak for the population
But peddling lies and their own delusion.
Social media reduces taking
Sides to like or dislike choices; insult
Is suppressed. Unless checks and balances
Exist stability has few chances.

Times Change.

Tinsel and paperchains used to be our decoration:
Now the season is dominated with flashing electrification.
Potted carol refrains ear-worm you in the shops
On an endless loop. Luminous Santas adorn rooftops.
Such horrors leading up to Christmas are commercial,
Advent forgotten, faith squeezed out and Christ child free
With the focus replaced by the tall Christmas tree.
The politically correct and mindful fearfully fall
Re-labelling the period "Winterval" but other faiths all
Take the opportunity to enjoy our native festival,
Its trappings and joys, holiday breathers and song.
In our secular world where have we gone wrong?
Why ashamed of our values as we shoulder the occasion
As for the kids but kid ourselves to face God with evasion.

Lazarus = Without Help.

Names betray a story, describe a situation,
Where a beggar maintained expectant station.
Starving at the rich man's gate begging a crust
None would help that could throw coins in the dust.
Then relieved and rewarded in the afterlife
Lazarus could only observe the rich man's strife.
Did our Lord neglect bringing His beloved friend relief
Missing entombment and facing his siblings' grief?
That Lazarus, unhelped too, found restoration
To Mary and Martha with Jesus' inclination.
Both are players in God's unfolding story
Whose respective sagas give God the glory
Showing that crossing over the great divide
There's more than comfort at Abraham's side.

Do Dreams Have Destinations?

As in a dream I seem never to arrive:
Life would appear as many destinations
Yet none for soon one moves on.
We hasten along but arrival's a con
As so many remain way stations
Down the line of being alive.
Just as Odysseus never reached home
Destined for ten years the seas to roam
So we encounter experiences
Discovering creation's sciences.
While once we used to dig and plough
Farming is so different now.
Yet our journey has a final stop,
Like seeds we know come death we drop.

Four poems based on Bampton Lecture 2022, Oxford University Church, by Prof. Alec Ryrie of Durham University; "The Age of Hitler, and how we can escape it."

Deep Silence.

What is heard listening to the silence
Like Elijah knew God's voice direct
His future ministry? Do wind stirred rushes
Like whispers generate a tale that pushes
Explanations none can correct
That Midas has asses' ears, hence
A source of enjoyed mythical nonsense.
Yet in the mind's quietness a consequence
Follows that clears the way ahead,
A course of action spirit led.
Like prayer is that other still small voice:
Answers come quietly and we rejoice.
Utter silence is a barrier to penetrate
To know the will of Him on whom we wait.

Moral Worth or Jubilee.[22]

Daleks would their view of Evil exterminate
Leaving evil over good to dominate.
Their moral worth such action denies
But then what criteria supplies
Our evaluation that concludes
Better sense than the present eludes?
Certain freedoms should be sacrosanct:
Speech and belief, no want, security
Guaranteed. Now, if God be thanked,
Shouldn't the world have greater maturity
Exposing charlatans, dictators and all?
Honor one another or else fall
Since letting go may seem a dream
But *shenat shemitah*[23] has much to redeem.

---

22. Hebrew: A year of letting go; a sabbatical year for people and creation.
23. A Hebrew name for the sabbatical year.

A Consideration of Good and Evil.

By what yardstick do we evaluate, assess
Our age or judge behavior, our human role?
Hitler the historical bogeyman
Replaced by rampant Putin both test
Human value systems regardless
Of divine truth initially given
To humankind to easily address
The worth of actions and leadership.
Wisdom is derived from weighing events;
Synthesis and discernment rest
On making an acceptable whole
That continues building our heritage.
Have we lost sight of that Christian glow
Given some two thousand years ago?

Propaganda v Humanity.

Rocks erode with continuous washing
By the surging sea yet that value
Outlined by Christ proud and weathered will stand
The test of time, monument to morality and
In life's storms a beacon of reality, true.
Hitler became the yardstick being
The bogeyman by which evil's measured,
Warning to all of any who truth denies.
Nonetheless there goes humanity
Hand-in-hand with humility
Whose expression on Christian roots relies
Prompting philanthropy by causes treasured,
Worthy of any Samaritan
Making the best response he can.

The Way of the World. (Apologetics!)

How come in this world of knowledge, research
Some seem so alone? Without reflections
Whatever the algorithms where's Wisdom?
To live well is a taste of Christendom
Not exotic holidays and distractions
In preference to Holy Days and Church
Being a reminder to the partaker
That earthly human insignificance
Is eclipsed getting to know our Maker
Who attaches to our lives such importance.
He gives us Light, a path to integrity
Diverting focus from self. Reality
'S solid spiritual dimension
Not our virtual world's wild abstraction.

Prompted Memory.

What but a store of facts recalled triggered
By other events, experiences,
People and what they might have said or done.
Store of past actions and past emotions
Colored by hindsight or something won:
Prompting photographs arouse former senses.
It all comes back as once you figured.
Been here before or false premonitions
Play havoc when things seem familiar
But then not quite as they were at the time?
Or are they fruits of a dream in the night?
Does recall grow with telling or all's right?
Do we view as second hand sublime
All that's past or just something similar?

The Lord's Prayer.

We acknowledge God as the source of life
Knowing we are in His kingdom when we
Do His will. There is His ample provision.
To forgive others isn't provisional:
It must not be hypocritical.
Well might we wonder if temptation
Is a stumbling block from God so that He
Can accuse us on judgment day for strife
Comes with a time of trial, but fast track
Christian belief leads to salvation
In this life sealed without improvisation
Anticipating no turning back.
Give God the glory, Father, Son, Spirit all three
Ever and always as One They shall be.

Four Rites of Passage.

Baptism.

Often mistaken for an act of thanks
After childbirth baptism is a beginning
Of a life's journey to a closer walk
With God. There is no map to replace talk
That gives direction and better meaning
To enable an undertaking that ranks
With order and reliance on that Light
That entered the world in human form.
In that light life is lived, our choices made
And self is left behind. No charade
Masks morals and values, rather a norm
Is established to discern wrong from right.
Symbolically washed sin's not erased
But forgiveness frees and let God be praised.

Holy Matrimony.

When God divided Adam to make Eve
From his rib to be his companion
He opened up His poetic creation
Setting in motion that future relation
Of husband and wife in a union
As one for their choice to achieve.
Freewill puts together God's division
Giving to His creation completion
In which man plays a part from the start.
From the beginning no revision
Was intended, yet God paid attention
To mankind's free choice and changes of heart.
The church blessing may not set a strong seal:
In view of human weakness there's appeal.

Death. Where To?

Blessed on our way, "May thy portion be in peace"
Could not be more true away from the clatter
Of this life which assumes we need a place
In a similar manner but in space
Amongst other worldly static chatter
Where departing souls take on a new lease:
"May thy dwelling be in the heavenly
Jerusalem." So what is this city?
Derived from a dream of better days,
Is heaven's finality devised
Where all our earthly mistakes are revised?
This one way last rite of passage conveys,
As we shuffle of this mortal coil, pity
In a grand finale aimed to be holy.

Burial. What is Holy?

Who can see beyond the crematorium
Curtain? Do our all hopes go up in smoke?
Are our prayers for the deceased in vain?
Surely death is our loss not theirs but gain
Of a whole new dimension for all folk
That's not confined to a church triforium!
Purged of our old earthly mortality
What's to be our new reality,
Intangible in this life despite desire
To discover the switch t'which we aspire?
Ageless, set apart, the mind much refined,
We share undeclined how God is defined:
When we are like Him we'll be able to see
Him as He is in heavenly glory.[24]

---

24. The last 2 lines pick up on 1 John 3,v2.

Let the Spirit Prompt.

In the stillness of silence find
By allowing the ear to hear
Or try to unpick the poet's mind
Until strange metaphors are clear.
So scripture slowly, quietly read
Unravels something of what God said.
All is a work of art as poems
Mirror marvels of Creation
Dispelling codes and theorems
For truth and realization
That faith and science go hand in hand
Without seeing t'other as contraband.
The still small voice lacks no power
Allowing our perception to flower.

Old York Today.

Thirty nine churches made York thrive;
Of these nineteen still survive.
Embedded faith kept folk alive
To see fair play and not to swyve.
No longer dens of ill repute,
Bars and shops remain—some cute.
Folk fill night club dives, eating houses,
Ruin evenings with loud carouses,
Many with more tattoo than clothing,
With some girls almost all exposing.
Church based charities homeless feed
Stepping in where they spot a need.
The old churches host stained glass displays,
Music centers, help, and well being days.

Temple Worship.

Columned temples attracted votive
Offerings of many kinds and hue.
Positioned arms of small figures
Illustrated adoration, true
Aspects of worship with gestures
Alphabet named, phi, tau and psi.
Sulfur fumes rising from the ground
In the shrine of Zeus almighty
High in the hills where terraces abound
Entranced the consulted female seer
To speak prophecies at Delphi,
But beware their ambiguity.
Such old original fastness
Saw later hermits seek remoteness.

Classical Greece Culture, Olympia

Might the profiles of the distant
Hills suggest familiar faces
Or illustrate those ancient myths?
Was Agamemnon a remarkable
Face to remember, his brother
Menelaus respected by all?
Was the Acropolis, high town,
Clustered round a threshing floor?
At Olympia measured peace
Ruled during a national truce
For the best men to win laurels
(Unless pilloried as cheats)
In a spiritual surrounding,
With philosophy abounding.

Olympia, Greece. The spring source was hallowed, bringing water to the area for baths. Site of ancient games, based on martial arts, where participants had to be at peace and those who cheated were pilloried. The race track and arena were to the right, gymnasium and other sports to the left beyond Zeus's and Hera's respective temples. 2024.

Six Laments for Palestine, one for Ukraine.

The World Looks On . . .

The slung stones that killed Goliath
Cannot prevail against armor
And bullets. Nor does the math
Of countless innocents abhor
The killing, wanton destruction,
Murder of women and children,
Along with demolition
Of homes and eviction of old men.
Like terriers on a rat hunt
In the woodshed or hen run
Israelis have a blood lust, punt
On gains while laying waste, make fun
Of Palestinian helpless hostility,
Ignoring grounds for neutrality.

A Solution of Kintsugi[25] Hope.
(Remapping the Holy Land.)

As only broken earthen fragments of a pot
Can be joined to become a mend, more
Than a fix, so Kintsugi's metal cannot
Enhance to restore better than before
Without gold: a more expensive story
Than the former whatever its glory.
So Palestine, riven and rubble-ized,
And Israel, usurping and over sized,
Need a golden weld to meld fractious
Parts creating that harmonious
Seam with peace the theme gained at a price
Purging anger's heat and revenge's ice.
That gold is supportive, international,
Christian, refining and rational.

25. Kintsugi = Japanese mending/improving broken china with gold.

Unfair on Gaza: No Safe Places Despite Warnings.

What of so many people displaced?
Netanyahu may be stern-faced
But lip-service and blatant lies
For excuses come as no surprise
In the wake of so much destruction
Claiming targets are reduction
Of hostile bunkers surveillance sourced
Regardless where civilians are forced
To flee and huddle within the ghetto.
Like a dog with a bone no let go
Is offered with humanity
Nor respite from the military.
Post despicable Hamas atrocity
Palestinians deserve some pity.

Gaza's Lament.
(For Those Who Mourn But Will The Other Side Listen?)

What memorial is Gaza's rubble
As mourning mothers scratch and scrubble
For their crushed children's corpses encased
In collapsed masonry, displaced
Themselves if they escaped the shells,
But none to mourn nor toll the bells
If they'd succumbed to such onslaught?
The world mourns what such hell has brought.
Such is the price Israel has sown
That Hamas has unleashed on its own,
But such revenge will fuel more;
No walls can contain wounds so raw.
Justice doesn't merit atrocity
Nor annihilation of a city.

Plight of the Palestinians.

When will a tide of justice flow
Like a local river in spate?
Or are such hopes dried up and low
Like a stream in a drought of late?
Too like those pilgrims come to learn
Holy Land sites but not unravel
That a Jubilee Year return
To restore all to a level,
The "acceptable year of the Lord,"
That Jesus taught was true release
For those caught in darkness to ward
Off slavery and oppression cease.
The land is God's, all men mere tenants
Placed to fulfill His commandments.

Indifference.

How can we stand indifferently by?
Innocents are slaughtered. Mothers cry
At man's inhumanity to man.
Is this part of any of God's plan?
Is the politicians' only interest
Not rooting for what's fair and best
But catching votes for the next election?
Surely the reason for their rejection
Is Gaza reduced to mounds of rubble.
Suffice to say war means more trouble!
We're taught perfect love casts out fear
So is peace more than they can bear?
Rather than take some supposed side
Only shared talk can bridge the divide.

There Can Be Hope in Context.

The sunflower is pollinated
So likely to flower anew,
But unmated bear won't continue
Despite having hibernated
If global warming still allows
Salmon run as seasonal food
Whilst river water flows
And Nature has a steady mood.
Wind can seed the flora, fauna
Will need sustenance to survive
Ere the earth shrivels to mourn a
Dearth of anything once alive
After man neglected his duties
To steward creation's beauties.

God in His Garden.

In the cool of the day God walked
In His garden taking His ease,
To encounter His humans who talked
And whose company was there to please.
This paradise was orderly
To the point of perfection:
Beauty had been prescribed early
To be different in each section.
So there were many mansions
Of character in this sizable House:
Colour, scent and taste, provisions
In themselves for Adam and spouse
Till their naked shame did destroy
God's expectation to share His joy.

Reflection and Familiarization of Isaiah 61:1-11.

After thought a passage for illumination
Looking to the future with anticipation
That God for Israel intends restoration
If she as a nation goes for transformation
After a period that earned her devastation.
To understand the prophecy's inspiration
God, after wilderness years, makes declaration,
Indeed He extends an invitation,
That Jesus with His divine imagination
Will live and teach a way out of desperation
And how we can become a new plantation
With a priestly role for every generation
Following repentance as a restored nation
In the light of receiving promised salvation.

Perichoresis—The Divine Dance.
(A Hint of Proverbs 8.)

The Trinity circles within its circle tight
To a silent tune that beckons a Word
That others hear to let in Holy Light
Chasing from Truth all shadows marked absurd.
In quietness darkness is dis-spelled, quiz
Not understanding how it's overcome
With no obvious opposite. Light is.
Darkness brooded o'er the deep mute and dumb
Until God spoke setting in motion
A beginning that led to creation.
Wheeling in a whirl wind arose to join
As Spirit what was begun while the Son
Fixed as a master craftsman what was made
Earth's orb mantled by stars in a cascade.

Where Are Faith, Hope And Charity?[26]

Are our three Abrahamic faiths earthbound
Caught 'tween heritage and inheritance
Traced from landed promise to long distant
Patriarchs amongst the many but scant
In waterless deserts or those who chance
Their arm behind rival cousins around
Whom there rise different fundamental
Values at odds within the whole? The world
Becomes their victims with rules so tied down.
Supposed path to water[27] isn't there to drown.
An empty tomb leaves no family, relics curled,
No traceable start in an unknown rental,
But such freedom a jump of faith requires
And access to a new kingdom acquires.

---

26. Also the names of the three biplanes available to defend Malta in WWII!
27. Sharia means "path to water."

Uncovering A Bigger Picture.

We struggle constrained by our culture
To find glimmerings of God from within
The fullness of His Being that, for sure,
In turn beyond our ken makes love spin.
Yet with keeping an open mind
We can enjoy what others find
To enrich our own understanding.
Despite a narrow approach conditioning
Dialogue can enlighten each
Bold enough to share their riches, teach
Insights, traditions and stories,
Illustrations, glimpses of glories.
Written and spoken, read, then awoken
The Word indwells, no mere token.

Life Everlasting.

There is no time in Heaven, an open door
That it is now and tomorrow evermore.
When that moment comes, a blip,
Destined to worship our worship
Will be in the everlasting light
Of what was our best moment bright
In earthly life, our best effort
Of Christian service that others caught.
Not frozen in time nor time standing still
But an everlasting that can only time fill.
We will be our own act of obedience,
Beyond the ken of any science,
As lasting praise before our Maker
Made in response to our Life Taker.

What Of The Temple Mount?

Temple-tied adherents of two faiths trudge
(For each the other's presence is a grudge)
To a broken wall or a threshing floor
(Of their entitlement the core)
That once stood on a windy ridge.
Between the two there is no bridge.
For lost values there's history longing
Which worldly cares swept away to nothing.
For a third in the middle there are no ties
(Even earthly sites are not without lies)
Wailing walls and golden domes past glory
Phases of a longer, earlier story
Since spelled as a directive Word from God
Who taking human form these parts trod.

Euthanasia I.

Some suicides from desperation
While others are courageous
So what of the consideration
Where life is no longer prosperous
For individuals whose faculties
Decline and fail and family ties
Stretched beyond measure mourn the living?
Where is the pain killing cocktail giving
Gentle relief to a sure gathering?
Some whistle blower seeking glory
Has curtailed that acceptable story
Announcing your loved one's departing.
Now let those who struggle with life choose
When failed health leaves nothing to lose.

Euthanasia II.

Whilst I may be God's gift to my parents
Life is His gift to me for Himself on a par
With whatever purposes remain in store.
Bach's music on various instruments
May be played, adapted to accordion, guitar,
Organ or choir. His genius and gift are the score.
Our calling is the welfare of others
So what of our own? Am I my own master?
When no longer myself can I choose bothers:
The husk I am is no longer all I was, a star,
The positive me is negative, value discharged.
Players terminate music played through, enlarged.
Some need help to be eased into life no doubt,
What indignities must I endure to be eased out?

Religio: Tethered or Bound? (Matthew 11:28-30.)

What freedoms do we know through faith?
Is it an anchor to hold avast
Like boats secured against the tide
Or a tether as a horse after a ride
Is secured to feed rather than cast
Free to forage in a field? What saith
Our Lord to guide us in our lives
Rather than bind as Pharisees
Tied up the people of their day?
Secure belief is the only way
That an ordinary life, without fees
Levied on the soul for control, strives
For peace in a world self absorbed
Or unlit adrift aimless and bored.

Finding The Glory. A Listening Church.

Yet take people as she finds,
Prepared to go against the flow
To weigh with God others' problems
By listening, offering prayer, spent
To soothe and focus troubled minds,
Echoing the psalmist without show
Surrounded with doubt as life hems
In the individual pent
As relentless anxiety grinds.
Where else then can anyone go
But find peace in Wisdom's gems
Stirring the still small voice, silent
Till glory replaces lament?

SE corner of Temple Mount with foundations of washing/purification area opened up. 1988.

www.ingramcontent.com/pod-product-compliance
Lightning Source LLC
Chambersburg PA
CBHW050139170426
43197CB00011B/1890